PICTORIAL HISTORY OF
SOUTH AFRICA

PICTORIAL HISTORY OF
SOUTH AFRICA

ANTONY PRESTON

Foreword by
Professor T R H Davenport

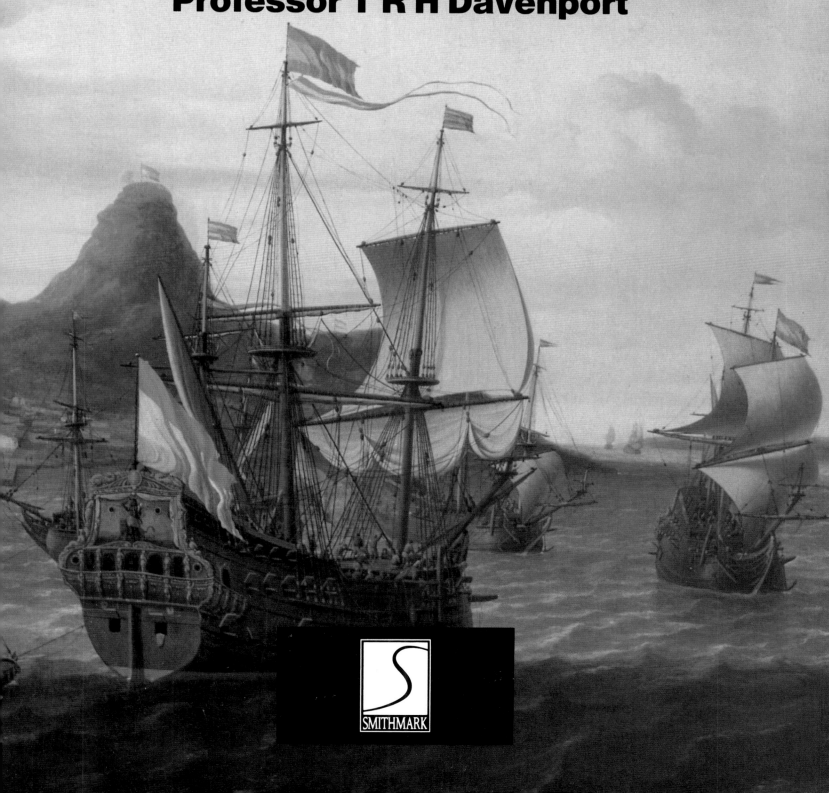

SMITHMARK

This edition published in 1995
by SMITHMARK Publishers Inc.,
16 East 32nd Street
New York, New York 10016

SMITHMARK books are available for bulk purchase for sales
promotion and premium use. For details write or telephone
the Manager of Special Sales, SMITHMARK Publishers Inc.,
16 East 32nd Street, New York, NY 10016. (212) 532-6600.

Produced by Brompton Books Corp.,
15 Sherwood Place
Greenwich, CT 06830

ISBN 0-8317-7081-3

Printed in China

10 9 8 7 6 5 4 3 2 1

Page 1: A Khoikhoi kraal on the
Orange River.

Pages 2-3: Table Bay in 1683, with
the *Africa* in the foreground.

FOREWORD BY PROFESSOR T R H DAVENPORT 6

PART I
EARLY SETTLERS AND PIONEERS

South Africa before the white man 10

Van Riebeeck and the Dutch settlers..........................14

New immigrants 16

The British take over the Cape....................................19

The settlement of Port Natal.......................................22

The empire of Shaka 25

The Great Trek 28
The origins

The Great Trek..31
The pioneers

The Great Trek 34
The massacre in Natal

The Great Trek 38
Retribution at Blood River

The settlers in Natal..42

The Boer Republics..45

Indian immigration...49

The diamond fields...52

PART II
ESTABLISHING THE REPUBLICS

Britain annexes the Transvaal.....................................60

The Zulu War...64
The invasion of Zululand

The Zulu War...70
The overthrow of Zulu military power

Paul Kruger 73

The First Anglo-Boer War 75
The causes of the conflict

The First Anglo-Boer War 79
Victory at Majuba

The discovery of gold 82

Cecil Rhodes 84

The Jameson Raid 88

The Second Anglo-Boer War 92
Opening shots

The Second Anglo-Boer War 95
Black Week

The Second Anglo-Boer War.......................................100
Destruction of the Republics

The Second Anglo-Boer War.......................................105
Attrition

The Second Anglo-Boer War.......................................108
To the bitter end

Rebuilding the nation 111

PART III
THE STRUGGLE FOR NATIONHOOD

Creating the Union of South Africa.............................116

The 1914 Rebellion 120

Jan Christiaan Smuts..122

The First World War..125
The conquest of South West Africa

The First World War..128
Fighting Lettow-Vorbeck

The First World War..130
Delville Wood

The Rand Rebellion 132

Rural depression 134

The Resurgence of Afrikanerdom................................138

The Second World War...140
South Africa goes to war again

The Second World War...143
'Up North'

The Second World War...146
Fighting in Italy

Peace and Reaction 150

PART IV
APARTHEID, ISOLATION AND FREEDOM

The new ascendancy...156

Separate development becomes a reality 160

South Africa becomes a republic 163

The road to isolation 166

The rise of black nationalism.....................................170

War beyond the borders 175

Namibia...179

Some minor reforms 182

Violence, santions and stalemate 186

The release of mandela...192

The path to reform..198

The year of elections 203

Index and Acknowledgements 207

FOREWORD

South Africa has more history than almost any other country of comparable age and size. This must be qualified. Identifiable human settlement goes back perhaps 25,000 years. The first pastoralists go back two thousand. The first Europeans to settle reached our shores in the mid-seventeenth century, not long after the first white settlement of America. They consisted at that stage mainly of Dutchmen, Frenchmen and Germans, whose descendants have come to be known collectively as Afrikaners. The British only arrived at the end of the eighteenth century, taking over the country at the end of the Napoleonic Wars. The first white settlers encountered the indigenous boskopoid pastoral hunter communities, traded with them, quarrelled with them, and with the help of superior weaponry took much of their land. By the end of the eighteenth century they had made contact with the Bantu-speaking negroid peoples in the region of present-day Port Elizabeth. By the end of the nineteenth, after a century marked by alternating conflict and cooperation, the Europeans had asserted their military and political control over the whole sub-continent. They had discovered diamonds and gold, set up market towns, and with the help of the local black labour which they could command, and the immigrant artisans whom they could attract, they had transformed a garden of Eden into a modernising industrial state. They had brought the plough, more potent forms of alcohol, manufactured clothing, firearms, literacy, new diseases and medical knowledge to cope with them, railways, and Christianity (which at first encountered much resistance on account of the inroads made by the missionaries into such practices as polygamy, but made significant advances in the post-conquest era).

The writing of South African history has gone through several stages. Until recently, very little of it has been written

by blacks – a fact easily attributable to the subordinate role to which they have been relegated in society. A Eurocentric, predominantly British perspective at first prevailed in our historical writing, and this led to a reaction among Afrikaners, who began to promote their own 'people's history'. Since the middle of the present century there has been a determination to 'decolonize' the writing of our history by ensuring that it is presented as the history of the entire South African people, black as well as white. A black 'people's history' is now beginning to appear. It overlaps with, and may at times run counter to, the history of the scholars.

Left: Zulu blacksmiths at work. First led by Shaka, the Zulus became the dominant black nation in southern Africa for much of the nineteenth century.

Above: Groote Schuur after the restoration carried out for Cecil Rhodes by Herbert Baker in the late 1890s.

Right: A painting by A Pavy entitled a *South African native bound for the goldfields* (1894).

South Africa is a country in travail, standing in the dock of world opinion, which has itself changed dramatically since a Eurocentric view gave place to broader perspectives in the international political market place. It is important, therefore, that those who write South African history should be informed by a desire to present the story so as to lead readers to an understanding of events as they really happened.

The writer of a pictorial history operates under certain constraints, but also enjoys certain real advantages. The chief limiting factor is that pictorial histories home in more easily on the actions rather than the thoughts and feelings of the people whose experiences constitute the essential story. The advantages consist mainly of the ease with which one can project visual images, which can communicate an accurate impression so much more quickly than the written word. That is the case with this book, which places a heavy emphasis on the major military conflicts in the South African past. It is my hope, therefore, that the reader will be inspired by what appears in these pages to develop a fascination for the history of this country in its broader aspects, because they touch on the central dilemmas of the wider world in so many ways. I like to think that he or she will move on to some of the works suggested for further reading, so that the number of people who are informed about the South African crisis may grow, and their influence come to dominate the decisions of the politicians inside and outside the country.

Antony Preston has himself lived in South Africa, and attended South African university. He claims descent from one of the great conciliators of South African history, General Sir William Butler, who did more than most people to try to prevent the outbreak of the Anglo-Boer War in 1899. In an easy and economical style, Antony Preston takes the reader through the action-dominated events of South African history, and I wish him success in his venture.

T R H DAVENPORT

PART I
EARLY SETTLERS AND PIONEERS

SOUTH AFRICA BEFORE THE WHITE MAN

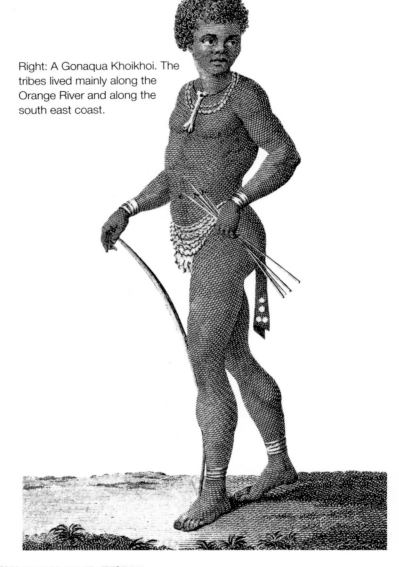

Right: A Gonaqua Khoikhoi. The tribes lived mainly along the Orange River and along the south east coast.

If the latest claims made by anthropologists prove to be correct, *Homo sapiens* appeared in southern Africa some scores of thousands of years earlier than in Europe and Asia. Scholars may argue about the precise dating but there is no doubt that the ancient theories of race — the four quarters of the globe occupied by red Americans, white Europeans, dark Asians and black Africans — are now discredited.

Recent scholarship has also rejected the former division of the indigenous inhabitants of the sub-continent into Bushmen and Hottentots. The term Khoikhoi or Khoi is now preferred for the Hottentot race, and their own term San for the Bushmen. This similarity in terminology underlines the similarities that exist between the two peoples.

What we do know from archaeological evidence is that as early as the tenth century the Khoikhoi appear to have owned sheep, and later they owned horned cattle. They were never very numerous, and by the mid-seventeenth century probably numbered no more than 100,000. The Khoikhoi were located mainly along the Orange River and along the coast from the south-western region of Africa to the Transkei in the south-east, but may at one time have lived in what is now Natal.

The San, on the other hand, living south of the Orange River, may never have exceeded 20,000 people. Their dependence on game forced them to be highly mobile, and to limit their patrilineal groups to no more than 200 at most. Their political organisation was rudimentary, and although chiefs were appointed as leaders they had no institutional authority.

It has long been held that the first Bantu-speaking people arrived on the highveld of the Transvaal at about the same time as the first white men arrived at the Cape, but modern archaeological evidence challenges this view. Radiocarbon dating of evidence suggests that Negroid Iron Age settlements in the Transvaal may date from before the fifth century AD. However these early settlements were probably part of an

Above right: Korah Khoikhoi dismantling huts to move to new grazing grounds. A coloured aquatint of 1805 by Samuel Daniell.

Right: Khoisan frying locusts, 1805. A coloured aquatint by Samuel Daniell.

Left: A Khoisan camp. They, like the San, probably did not exceed 20,000, and lived in groups of less than 200.

Previous pages: *A Kaffer village*, 1804, a coloured aquatint by Samuel Daniell.

Above: Bartolomeu Dias de Novaes sailed from Lisbon in August 1487 with two caravels and a storeship and rounded the Cape five months later.

ebb and flow of small groups, rather than a mass movement.

Growing population and prosperity probably combined to force the Bantu people southward. The introduction of maize, for example, enabled the land to support more people. The natural barrier of the Kalahari Desert to the west and the scourge of the tsetse fly in the Limpopo valley together acted as a funnel, pushing settlers south to the highveld where they could rear large herds of cattle, and to the good grazing pastures of the coastal hinterland.

The Bantu-speaking settlers fell into three main groups. The Ovambo and Herero tribes moved from the Congo Basin into the south-west region of Africa, the Shona-speaking chiefdoms moved into the area between the Limpopo and the Zambezi rivers, while the remaining tribes moved south of the

Limpopo into the land we know today as the Republic of South Africa.

The country was not to remain isolated indefinitely. Between 1405 and 1433 the Chinese· admiral Cheng-ho made seven voyages into the Indian Ocean, reaching East Africa. Had Cheng-ho not died suddenly in 1434 it is quite feasible that he might have pressed on to the south, but with his death the Chinese lost interest in maritime expansion.

The discovery of South Africa was left to the Portuguese, who sought a route to the East where they traded in spices. Bartolomeu Dias rounded the *Cabo da Boa Esperanca* (Cape of Good Hope) in 1488, while Dom Pero de Covilha, sailing southwards from Ethiopia, reached the mouth of the Zambezi. Dias and his men made a landing at Fish Bay near the Gourits River, where they saw Khoikhoi herdsmen for the first time, and went on to Mossel Bay. By the time they reached *Bahia de Lago* (Delagoa Bay) the crews were exhausted and Dias was forced to return home via a circuitous route after reaching the Keiskamma River.

In 1497 Vasco da Gama sailed on a further expedition to the Indies, and this time he achieved success, arriving at Calicut in India in May 1498. He and his caravels made a landfall at St Helena Bay in November 1497. The Portuguese also had their first fatal encounter with the Khoikhoi, when da Gama and some of his companions received spear-wounds. The Cape of Good Hope was rounded on 22 November and a second landing was made in Mossel Bay. On Christmas Day the four caravels reached the Pondoland coast, and to commemorate the occasion da Gama named the coast Natal. The coast of South Africa was now known to mariners, however little was known of the hinterland.

Below: The Portuguese artist F Benda made this oil painting of the planting of the *Padrão São Filipe* at Cape Maclear on 6 June 1488, one of three stone crosses erected by Dias.

Right: Vasco da Gama left Portugal in July 1497 with four ships, and landed at Mossel Bay in November before going on to India.

VAN RIEBEECK AND THE DUTCH SETTLERS

The Portuguese had little interest in the hinterland of South Africa, but as their trade with India developed during the sixteenth century the Cape coast provided useful landfalls for picking up fresh water and food, and resting places where sick seamen could recover. As Portugal's strength declined other nations started to use the Cape route. The first Englishman to round the Cape was Francis Drake in 1580, on his way back to England after circumnavigating the globe, and in 1595 the first Dutch fleet dropped anchor in Mossel Bay.

Although the French and the Danes both tried to exploit the wealth of the East Indies it was the English who first thought of establishing a permanent settlement at the Cape in 1620. But King James I showed no interest in the project, and it was left to the Dutch to take the first steps.

In 1650 the Lords Seventeen of the Dutch East India Company decided to establish a fortified station at the Cape, to facilitate trade with the East Indies by offering the Company's ships and men some respite on their long voyages between the Netherlands and the Indies.

The man chosen to run the new settlement was Jan van Riebeeck. Born in 1619 in Culemborg in the Netherlands, he served as a ship's surgeon and later as a Company employee in Batavia. His instructions were to build a fort, to improve Table Bay as an anchorage, to plant a garden for fresh vegetables and fruit, and to acquire livestock by barter with the local inhabitants.

The ten years of van Riebeeck's rule lasted from 1652 to 1662, and were modestly successful. A jetty was built in Table Bay to reduce the hazards of landing, but the small mud fort was quite inadequate to defend the settlement. Agricultural production lagged behind the needs of passing ships, largely because the tiny garrison could not perform all the tasks

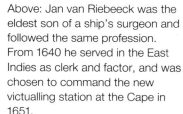

Above: Jan van Riebeeck was the eldest son of a ship's surgeon and followed the same profession. From 1640 he served in the East Indies as clerk and factor, and was chosen to command the new victualling station at the Cape in 1651.

Left: A Khoikhoi village at Table Bay, from a 1711 engraving in Abraham Bogaert's *Historische Reizen*. The cow on the left is being insufflated anally to help milking.

Left: Jan van Riebeeck landed at Table Bay in April 1652, charged with the duty of victualling and assisting the Company ships trading with the East Indies.

Below: The first land grant to a free burgher, in favour of Jakob Cloete of Cologne. The grant, dated 1657, refers to land on the Liesbeek River.

demanded of it. When van Riebeeck sailed for Batavia in 1662 to take up his next post he left behind a Dutch community of about 260 burghers, officials and dependents. To eke out the shortage of manpower the first slaves had already been imported from Batavia.

Colonial society was hierarchical, with the Governor at its head. His officials included the Deputy Governor, the garrison commander, various administrators and the Fiscal. This last-named official was responsible for tackling corruption, and from 1690 he answered directly to the Lords Seventeen. However his exactions caused great friction, and in 1793 his independent role was terminated.

Below the Governor's circle were the rank-and-file. Most were soldiers or sailors, but there were also artisans and farmers among them. The East India Company never restricted the recruiting of officials or lowly employees to Dutchmen, and so the colonists included Swiss, Germans, Scandinavians, Flemings and French. Until 1780 the Calvinist Dutch Reformed Church was the only branch of religion tolerated, but thereafter the Lutherans were permitted to worship as well. Other religions had to rely for religious comfort on priests or chaplains in passing ships.

As in other small communities promotion was slow, and one of the few ways of escaping the drudgery and dull routine was a temporary release to work for a farmer as a *knecht* (serf). This could eventually be turned into a permanent discharge, with the ex-employee becoming a 'free burgher'. In 1660 there were some 120 free burghers, but by 1745 there were more than 1000; by the end of the eighteenth century the figure had doubled, and there were seven or eight to every Company employee.

The Company had never intended to allow its small out-station to become a colony but growth was inevitable. As early as 1657 the decision to rely on the free burghers for food tied the Company's hands in its attempts to regulate daily life. Expeditions to the interior and the conversion of pastures to cultivated land inevitably caused friction between the settlers and the Khoikhoi, who recognised the threat to their traditional grazing and hunting grounds.

NEW IMMIGRANTS

The Revocation of the Edict of Nantes by King Louis XIV in 1685 forced many Protestant Huguenots to leave France. Many took advantage of the East India Company's offer of a free passage to the Cape of Good Hope, so marking the first sizeable transfusion of new blood into the tiny colony. Some 225 Huguenot refugees started to arrive from 1688, and were granted land at Drakenstein in the Berg River valley.

Each settler received agricultural implements, seed and cattle as a repayable loan. Many had brought with them vine-cuttings, and with these established vineyards that flourished. The cold wet winters and long dry summers, very similar to climatic conditions in southern France, helped to lay the foundations of today's wine and brandy export trade.

Despite the influx of Huguenots the colony remained Dutch in character. Governor Simon van der Stel dispersed the new settlers along the Berg River valley, and required them to communicate as far as possible in Dutch. Similarly the small number of German settlers who came to the Cape in the eighteenth century never established themselves as a distinct community despite outnumbering the new Dutch immigrants

The first slaves were imported from Angola and West Africa as early as 1658, but subsequently they were brought from the East coast. By the early eighteenth century slaves outnumbered the white settlers.

Some of the early settlers had taken Khoikhoi women as wives but in 1685 such white-black marriages were forbidden. Although the Company had doubts about the debilitating effect of slave-owning on the Cape settlers, and a 'white labour' policy was proposed as early as 1716, the practice was allowed to continue.

Severe punishments were prescribed by the High Court for slaves who tried to escape or assaulted their owners. Domestic slaves, on the other hand, were usually better treated and were encouraged to become artisans and craftsmen. A slave could earn his freedom by conversion to Christianity, or could purchase it.

The arrival of a new Governor in October 1679 marked a turning point in the fortunes of the infant colony. Simon van der Stel had orders to promote the well-being of the settlement, and he introduced a freehold system of land tenure at Stellen-

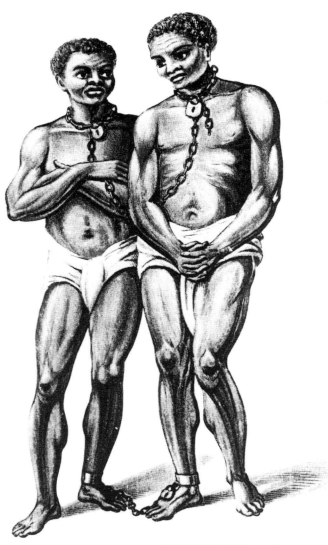

bosch. This proved successful and was extended to a new settlement at Drakenstein seven years later. The process continued in areas opened to farming by van der Stel's son Willem Adriaan, as late as 1717.

The drawbacks were soon apparent. Too many settlers meant over-production and consequent hardship for the smaller farmers. Some settlers prospered by retaining the profitable monopolies of wine, beer and meat, but others went to the wall. The choice was then between moving back into Cape Town or out into the interior.

The growing prosperity of the port created what are known today as service industries, catering for the needs of seafarers and the wealthy burghers, many of whom lived in Cape Town. For those who chose the interior there was the attraction of

Above: Black slaves chained together at the neck and ankles. There were more than 17,000 slaves at the Cape by the end of the eighteenth century.

Above right: Vergelegen, the homestead of Governor Willem Adriaan van der Stel. His success attracted the envy of the free burghers, who accused him of tyranny and profiteering.

Left: Stellenbosch in 1779, as seen by Samuel Davis, an Indian civil servant who visited the Cape.

Right: *Journeying Kaffirs*, an aquatint from Alberti's *De Kaffers*, published in 1810.

Above: This oil painting is of the Dutch ship *de Vis*, wrecked in Table Bay in 1740. Mariners soon nicknamed the Cape of Good Hope the Cape of Storms.

Right: Greenmarket Square in 1764, showing (left) a slave returning from a flogging and (right) a sedan chair.

stock-farming. Herds of livestock could be built up with no great capital outlay, with less labour and no need to transport perishables over bad roads.

These 'trekboers' were encouraged by the issue of free grazing permits under the rule of Willem Adriaan van der Stel. Not even the imposition of a small fee from 1714 could stop the movement, as farmers looked for new pastures.

Try as the Company might, it could not limit expansion. Stellenbosch had been recognised as a separate settlement in 1682; Swellendam followed in 1745 and Graaff-Reinet in 1786. Friction was inevitable between the sturdy, independent burghers and the Company ruled by restrictive bureaucracy. Throughout the eighteenth century this tension grew, until Company rule ended in 1795.

Criticism of official privileges sparked off the Burgher Protest of 1705-07, when the Governor was accused of manipulating the market for private gain. As late as 1778 the Cape Patriots were demanding an end to restrictions on trade.

The 'open' frontier was a bone of contention between the trekboers and the Xhosa tribes. Governor von Plettenberg's attempt to define a new boundary along the Fish River met with no success. Two pastoral and hunting groups, each adhering to its own distinct system of land tenure, were bound to clash. Attempts by the Company to conciliate the Xhosa outraged the farmers, and the first of a new series of 'frontier wars' began.

THE BRITISH TAKE OVER THE CAPE

Events in Europe were to transform the nature of the Cape Colony. In January 1795 a French revolutionary army invaded the Netherlands; the Batavian Republic was proclaimed and Prince William of Orange was forced into exile in England. By the end of the year the Dutch East India Company was under state control, a shadow of its former self.

Great Britain, arming herself against the rising tide of revolution and Jacobinism, had no intention of allowing the Cape of Good Hope to fall into French hands. Using the pretext of securing the Cape for the House of Orange, troops under Major General Craig took possession of the Colony in September 1795. Opposition was half-hearted and Commissioner-General Sluysken capitulated when the burghers of Graaff-Reinet refused his call for support.

Left: Commodore Sir Home Popham commanded the British fleet which occupied the Cape in 1806.

Above: A late Victorian view of Major General Craig's occupation of the Cape in 1795 in the name of the Prince of Orange.

The occupation ended in 1803, when the Cape was handed back to the Batavian Republic to comply with the Treaty of Amiens. In 1806 the British returned, but this time their 'temporary' stay became permanent. In 1814 as part of a general redistribution of colonies and possessions, the Cape was ceded to Great Britain.

At first British rule made hardly any difference to life at the Cape. The new rulers had no desire to precipitate a rebellion, and did little to alter the existing legal framework. Roman-Dutch Law remained the basis of the system and all property rights were guaranteed, but a start was made on eradicating the old monopolies. In fact the Batavian Government of 1803-06 had already achieved considerable reforms, improving the administrative machinery and relaxing the laws on religion and education. But the main problem, friction between the frontier farmers and the Xhosa, was not tackled.

The British soon found that they could not ignore the frontier problems, and the Fourth Frontier War of 1811-12 forced the Administration to build military posts, including the garrison towns of Cradock and Grahamstown. A more lasting solution was increased European settlement on the

Above left: *All among the Hottentota capering ashore*, a satirical view of the 1820 settlers by Cruickshank reminding migrants of the dangers on land.

Left: Settlers landing in surf boats at Algoa Bay. A thousand families were settled in the eastern Cape partly to relieve unemployment in Britain and partly to provide defenders for the frontier.

Above: An aquatint of Governor Janssens meeting the Xhosa chief Ngqika at the Kat River in 1803, bringing the Third Frontier War to an end.

Right: Lord Charles Somerset became Governor of the Cape in 1814. His autocratic style angered the colonists but he did much to improve the well-being of the colony.

they were in no sense paupers. Articulate and literate, they showed the same resilience to natural disasters as the Dutch before them, and the same sturdy independence.

In 1820 5000 British settlers reached the Cape. Unlike the Huguenots who were scattered and diffused, the 1820 settlers were all given 100-acre lots in the Zuurveld. The Governor, Lord Charles Somerset pursued a policy of Anglicisation, encouraging the new settlers to put down roots and to retain their sense of national identity. The Cape Colony was now part of the British Empire, which supplied much more economic dynamism than had ever been possible under Dutch rule. Great Britain was building a worldwide commercial empire based on the doctrines of free trade. Her textile mills provided a ready market for Cape wool and the Spanish merino sheep was imported to improve the local breed.

Not all the reforms were welcome. In 1815 a rebellion broke out at Slagter's Nek when a local farmer Frederik Bezuidenhout refused to attend court to answer charges of cruelty to one of his Khoikhoi servants. An attempt to arrest Bezuidenhout led to an exchange of fire in which he was killed, and his brother swore vengeance.

Unwisely Johannes Bezuidenhout invited the Xhosa chief Ngqika to support his rebellion, and the uprising was vigorously suppressed. The rebels were hanged at Slagter's Nek, but the executions were bungled. After the ropes broke the unfortunates were hanged a second time, creating the first of many martyrs for the cause of independence.

By allying themselves with Ngqika the Slagter's Nek rebels had alienated the majority of frontiersmen. Nevertheless the unnecessary harshness of the authorities came as a shock to farmers accustomed, after many years under Company rule, to taking the law into their own hands.

Eastern frontier. In 1819 the British Government introduced an immigration scheme under which some 4000 people, mostly farmers, artisans and ex-soldiers, were granted land in the Zuurveld on the western side of the Great Fish River. Many had become unemployed in the post-war recession but

THE SETTLEMENT OF PORT NATAL

The first white traders settled at Port Natal in 1824, hoping to win a share of the profitable ivory trade already passing through the Portuguese settlement at Delagoa Bay. The first group, led by a young Englishman, Henry Francis Fynn, soon realised that the whole of 'Independent Kaffraria' was virtually the property of the Zulu king Shaka.

Luckily for the settlers, their emissaries to Kwa Bulawayo aroused the Zulu monarch's curiosity, and when Fynn helped to nurse Shaka back to health his position was assured.

The little settlement at Port Natal grew largely through the efforts of Captain Allan Francis Gardiner, a missionary zealot who failed in his attempts to preach the Gospel among the Zulus, but whose energy as magistrate helped to transform the settlement into a thriving town. A school was the first sign of civilisation, followed by a formal street plan. In June 1835 the settlers adopted the name d'Urban in honour of the Governor of the Cape Sir Benjamin d'Urban, but the apostrophe was soon dropped.

Like Shaka before him, Dingane treated the Europeans like minor chieftains; he offered Gardiner control over all European traders entering Zululand. Although fooled into accepting the offer Gardiner was clever enough to realise that he could not make the arrangement work without real power. He

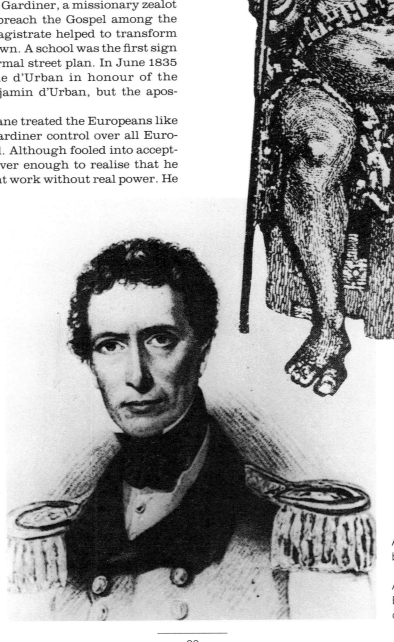

Above: Henry Francis Fynn initiated the development of Port Natal.

Right: Captain Allan Gardiner failed in his missionary work with the Zulus but transformed Port Natal into a thriving settlement.

Above: Dingane, Shaka's half-brother.

Above right: Major General Sir Benjamin d'Urban was Governor of the Cape from January 1834.

asked Sir Benjamin d'Urban to annex the whole of Natal and to appoint officials. Flattered, the Governor wrote to Dingane to confirm the new arrangement, but decided against complete annexation.

A steady trickle of settlers began to reach Durban by 1836, but the lack of central authority produced something close to anarchy. When Piet Retief and 15 companions arrived in October 1837 he was welcomed, and there was talk of Anglo-Boer co-operation. The situation was truly chaotic; the British Government had no wish to annex Natal, which was seen as

Dingane's kingdom, yet in theory every Boer and every Briton was a British subject. The Britons would have acknowledged Crown rule if it had been exercised, but the Boers would not.

Retief wanted a Boer republic but he was willing to accept the British settlers' control of Durban as it would provide his own people with a port. The British could be left in peace to develop all the communal facilities which the Boers needed but were disinclined to do for themselves.

The massacre of the Boer settlers and the Battle of Blood River removed any dreams of peaceful development. In fact

Above: General Sir George Napier, KCB, succeeded d'Urban as Governor in 1838.

Right: Coloured lithograph of a *Kraal on the Umgeni* with cattle and sheep.

Below: Coloured lithograph of Port Natal, later renamed Durban in honour of the Governor of the Cape.

the settlers at Durban were the first to warn the Boers of the impending attack but they arrived too late. Without waiting for Boer reinforcements they organised a successful attack on Zulu kraals, using friendly Izinkumbi warriors, but a second foray was badly mauled. Alarmed by reports of anarchy and bloodshed, the new Governor of the Cape Sir George Napier sent troops to Durban to restore order and to offer some relief to the victims of the massacre.

For their part the Boers laid out their own capital, named Pietermaritzburg to honour Piet Retief and Gerrit Maritz. Sadly, the title of the 'Free Province of New Holland in South East Africa' conveyed a misleading impression; the Volksraad was much given to disputation and high-flown declarations but its Treasury remained obstinately bankrupt.

The British Government, conforming to its policy, withdrew its troops at the end of 1839, a signal to the Boers to hoist their flag over Durban. Dingane was confronted, and in a series of raids the commandos confiscated some 60,000 head of cattle. Dingane fled only to be murdered, and the leadership of his nation passed into the hands of the compliant Mpande.

With the British gone, apparently for good, and the Zulus defeated there was abundant land, as well as cattle and cheap labour. Here at last was the *lekker lewe* (good life), for which so many had worked. The Government of the infant republic might be incompetent and the Volksraad impotent but the morrow would take care of itself.

THE EMPIRE OF SHAKA

To understand the rise of Shaka and the Zulu nation it is essential to take into account a huge upheaval among the Bantu-speaking peoples, comparable in its effect to the two world wars. To the Nguni-speaking peoples it was known as *Mfecane*, to the Sotho-speakers it was *Difaqane* or *Lifaqane*, but the meaning was similar: a 'crushing' or 'hammering' or 'forced migration'. This series of population shifts occurred during the second decade of the nineteenth century, and all historians agree that its scale was vast, and that it exerted a major impact on developments in southern Africa during the first half of the nineteenth century.

The precise origins are impossible to verify; the Bantu provided only an oral tradition, and credulous missionaries and travellers, unfamiliar with the pattern of tribal life, tended to distort what they were told. But we do know that towards the end of the eighteenth century loose confederations began to form, and among the largest were the Mthethwa under Dingiswayo, the Ndwandwe under Zwide and the Ngwane under Sobhuza. Dingiswayo developed his people's military efficiency, and started to consolidate an empire south of the White Umfolozi River.

One of the clans in the Mthethwa confederation was the Zulu clan, the 'People of the Heavens'. The Zulus passed under the yoke as a result of a brilliant victory in which a young regimental commander Shaka and his *iziCwe* regiment had beaten their neighbours. In 1816 Dingiswayo appointed the tall 29-year-old warrior to succeed his father as chief of the Zulus.

Under his brilliant leadership the small, demoralised clan was groomed for greatness. The military tactics he had per-

Above: Coloured lithograph of *Mtimuni, nephew of Shaka*, who carries a Nguni-type shield and the short stabbing assegai, the *iKlwa* pioneered by Shaka in his reshaping of traditional Nguni tactics.

Left: Coloured lithograph of spotted hyaenas and vultures feeding on carcasses in the wake of Shaka's *impis*. Shaka's reign rapidly degenerated into one of arbitrary power and bloodlust.

Left: A young Zulu warrior, photographed in 1860. All males under the age of 40 were conscripted into three age regiments, each with distinct headdresses and shields.

Right: A late Victorian view of the meeting between Lieutenant Farewell and Shaka. First contacts with white ivory hunters started in 1824.

fected with the *iziCwe* were taught, particularly his skill with the *iKlwa*, the short stabbing assegai. He formed four regiments, the minimum to allow him to use his tactics of the 'horns', 'loins' and 'chest'. The two horns raced out to surround the enemy *impi*, then the chest, the strongest force, engaged frontally. The loins formed a reserve, sitting with their backs to the battle until needed. What marked Shaka's army was its unequalled ability to carry out these complex movements silently, fast and with perfect alignment, even when running barefoot over broken ground.

Shaka built up his empire carefully, well aware that the Mthethwa could crush him if he became a threat to their hegemony. His first important victory destroyed the Butelezi clan but Shaka was careful to send the captured cattle to Dingiswayo.

Shaka's moment came in 1818, when Zwide's army defeated Dingiswayo; the Mthethwa chieftain was captured before the battle, and his leaderless army lost heart. The Zulus had been delayed, and only their steadiness enabled the survivors to escape. Thereafter the Mthethwa influence declined, but the Zulus prospered. At the Battle of Gqokoli Hill Shaka's forces drove off the Ndwandwe. In May 1819 Zwide invaded Zulu territory once more but this time his army was destroyed. In only three years Shaka had conquered territory larger than

the original Mthethwa confederation; 100 square miles of territory was now 11,500 square miles and the army now numbered 20,000.

Shaka was less wise than Dingiswayo had been. His *impis* now conquered and destroyed at will. By 1824 there was no longer any clan in the area south of the Thukela River. To the north the picture was the same, and the debris of smashed clans contributed to the huge movement of *Mfecane* as the survivors fled to avoid the Zulu wrath.

Absolute power destroyed Shaka, but not before his bloodlust had turned on his own people. Witnesses wrote of the endless and apparently meaningless killings. The death of Shaka's mother Nandi unleashed another reign of terror – 7000 Zulus were killed on the day that she died – and plotters finally plucked up courage to bring the madness to an end. Shaka's half-brothers Dingane and Mhlangana and an *induna* (tribal elder) called Mbopa stabbed him on 22 September 1828. He was probably 41 years old, and had ruled only 12 years. Shaka had created a great nation but at the cost of destroying the way of life of the Bantu-speaking peoples forever. As a result of the widespread warfare an estimated two million people had died (some authorities claim that this figure is an exaggeration); power was now concentrated in a few mighty warrior-chiefdoms – the Basuto, Matabele, Swazi and Zulu.

THE GREAT TREK
THE ORIGINS

Continuing friction on the eastern frontier of the Cape Colony between the white stock farmers and the Xhosa over the possession of land became acute in the early nineteenth century. The sparsely populated frontier was impossible to police with the resources available, and yet the Government was understandably unwilling to permit the farmers to take the law into their own hands.

The frontier wars cost the frontline Boers serious losses, and after the Sixth Frontier War of 1834-35 discontent was at a new height. Many felt that farming on the eastern border was no longer profitable; a man could lose his life's work but still had to pay taxes. There was also a land shortage in the 1820s and 1830s; the white population was expanding, and every adult Boer male, contemptuous of the very idea of working for another, demanded land as a right.

With land prices rising and drought making life hard for those who already owned it, the pastoral life was becoming harder to achieve. There was also a shortage of labour which was exacerbated by Government measures to regularise relations between master and servant.

Small wonder that the vast hinterland looked so tempting. The trekboers had already shown that game and grazing were plentiful, and their sturdy independence did much to shape the attitudes of the frontier farmers.

Making matters worse were thousands of fugitives from the *Mfecane* who were entering the eastern and north-eastern districts. Some could be absorbed as servants or labourers but thousands more roamed at large – a source of tension.

The emancipation of slaves was the last straw, although there were comparatively few slaves in the eastern Cape. Many Afrikaners felt an increasing sense of political impotence, and Louis Tregardt, for example, complained that the Government 'compelled the Afrikaners to be soldiers'.

Above: Hintsa, paramount chief of the Xhosa, was captured during the Sixth Frontier War (1834-35). He was later shot while attempting to escape.

Above right: Khoisan cattle-thieves with farmers in pursuit, c1836. One animal is being killed to delay the pursuers.

Left: A Boer commando. The duty of each citizen to provide a firearm and a horse for mutual defence was made compulsory in 1739, but survived as a way of life long after Company rule ended.

Right: Commandant Rademeyer and ten men from the George Commando fighting off a Xhosa attack in a kloof on the Fish River in March 1835.

There were deeper spiritual and psychological causes. Piet Retief's famous Manifesto summed it up:

We despair of saving this country from the potential threat posed by the seditious and dishonest behaviour of vagrants, who have been allowed to spread over all parts of the country; nor do we see any prospects of peace or contentment in a country in which internal dissension is so rife.

His niece Anna Steenkamp spelled it out even more clearly:

. . . it was not so much the emancipation which drove us away as [the slaves] being placed on an equal footing with Christians, contrary to the laws of God and the natural differentiations of origins and faith. That it was unendurable for every decent Christian to bow down under such a burden was the reason we preferred to leave, so as to be better able to preserve the purity of our faith and doctrine.

Mass migration offered an apparently simple solution to all the problems. It offered free land, cheap labour, freedom from irksome central government regulations, good hunting and freedom of worship, but it also offered a 'proper relationship' between blacks and whites.

Although the resulting Great Trek was at one time hailed as the vanguard of Afrikaner nationalism, it has been criticised for its unhappy consequences. On the positive side it brought huge tracts of southern Africa under western European influence, but it undoubtedly divided the two white races at a crucial stage in the development of the Cape Colony and Natal, and hardened white racial attitudes. Despite petty regulations and shortage of resources, the Cape Government was working to improve the lot of its inhabitants. Within the limits of contemporary racial perceptions, the spirit of the times favoured reform and, even if not voting rights for all, at least some framework of legal safeguards to protect the weak against the strong.

Above: *The freed slave*, as seen by F T l'Ons, holds a document believed to be the 'General Order' of abolition promulgated in 1833.

Below: A Boer ox wagon, typical of those used later on the Great Trek. The entire structure could be broken down for man-handling over rugged terrain.

THE GREAT TREK
THE PIONEERS

The frontier farmers had laid their plans for the exodus with great care. As early as 1834 three *kommissie* treks were sent out to explore and report back on the interior. The most important of these, under Pieter Uys, reached Port Natal where it reported on the suitability of Natal for settlement. In 1835 Louis Tregardt and Hans van Rensburg left to explore what we now know as the Transvaal lowveld and Portuguese East Africa.

Tregardt was the first of the pioneering Afrikaner *Voortrekkers* who migrated from the Cape Colony in the 1830s. By September 1836 his party had reached the Zoutpansberg, and nearly a year later they began an arduous journey to the coast. A total of '46 Christians and seven servants' reached Delagoa Bay the following April, but Tregardt and his wife died of malaria. His diary is of great importance to the history of the Great Trek, for he was the only leader to record events on a day-by-day basis.

Andries Potgieter set off with his party at the end of 1835 or early in the New Year, heading north. In August 1836 they

Above: Louis Tregardt's wagon is brought down Wit Rivier Poort, an incident recorded in his diary of 1837. The sketch was made by W H Coetzer.

were north of the Vaal, where they encountered the Ndebele (rendered 'Matabele' in Sotho) under their formidable chief Mzilikazi. At the Battle of Vegkop on 16 October Potgieter's laager repulsed the Ndebele attack with heavy loss, and three months later the trekkers destroyed Mzilikazi's kraal at Mosega. The defeated tribe withdrew to the north to carve out a new territory north of the Limpopo.

Gert Maritz, a successful wagonmaker from Graaff-Reinet, led another party from the Cape in September 1836. His arrival in 'Transorangia' put new heart into the trekkers who had reached the area earlier and were in need of his administrative abilities. A provisional administration was established at Thaba Nchu, with a burgher council of seven. Maritz was elected President and Judge, while Potgieter was 'Laager Commandant' or military chief.

Piet Retief had emerged as a spokesman for the frontier farmers, and when he arrived with a large party of trekkers in Transorangia in April 1837 the community was further strengthened. Retief was soon elected Governor and supreme military commander, while Maritz remained Judge and President of the Council of Policy. However, squabbling soon broke out; with so many individualists, each from a different district, personality clashes were inevitable.

The main argument was over the destination of the Great Trek. Retief, Maritz and Uys wanted to go to Natal where they recognised the value of Port Natal as an outlet to the world, whereas Potgieter wanted to go north, to get as far away from British influence as possible. In the event they did both, for it was necessary to defeat the Ndebele to open the Transvaal.

Left: Piet Retief published his Manifesto in Grahamstown in 1837, listing the reasons why some Boers wished to leave the Cape Colony.

Below: Trekkers felling trees to ease the descent of wagons over rough terrain.

Left: In the Battle of Vegkop in October 1836 about 40 Boer men, women, children and servants defeated about 6000 Ndebele warriors.

Below left: Boer wagons descending Mackay's Nek, with wheels chained and men dragging on *riems* (rawhide thongs).

Below right: Andries Pretorius showed rare strategic and tactical skill when planning his revenge on the Zulus.

Religion was also a cause of dissent. The Cape Synod had not supported the Trek, and as no minister of the Dutch Church was prepared to accompany the trekkers it was necessary to appoint someone else to minister to their spiritual needs. Erasmus Smit, a former missionary and brother-in-law of Maritz, was the choice of Retief, but his fondness for liquor and his poor health did not commend him to a large number of trekkers. Potgieter's followers preferred the Wesleyan missionary James Archbell.

Overshadowed by the early leaders, Andries Pretorius was to be the saviour of the trekkers. When the winter of 1838 carried off many victims, dissent broke out. The death of Gert Maritz had removed a powerful personality, and a disenchanted Andries Potgieter withdrew with his followers, to pursue his goal of a northern republic on the highveld.

Pretorius was no stranger to the trekkers, for he had served as a scout in Transorangia, Natal and the Transvaal. In their desperation the trekkers appointed him Commandant-General on 25 November 1837. It was an exceptionally wise choice, for Pretorius was a talented leader and had considerable military skill.

The new Commandant-General recognised that the traditional Boer-mounted commando tactics would not work against a Zulu army, and chose instead the concept of a reinforced wagon laager. He also inculcated obedience and discipline among his men, and conveyed a sense of boundless optimism, both essential ingredients in his brilliant victory at Blood River.

THE GREAT TREK
THE MASSACRE IN NATAL

In October 1837 Piet Retief trekked to Natal to open negotiations with the English settlers at Port Natal and with the Zulu king Dingane, with a view to establishing a Boer republic of Natalia.

At first the trekkers were well received by Dingane but Retief misread the signs. The treacherous Zulu monarch was in fact very frightened, for these were the people who had defeated Mzilikazi and his Ndebele. Retief's request for permission to settle large numbers of Boers in Natal merely confirmed Dingane's fears, but to buy time he agreed to a compromise. If Retief would recover 300 stolen cattle from the chieftain Sikonyela, he could have the land he wanted.

Dingane had already decided to kill Retief but the chosen assassin refused to carry out the deed, and tried to escape to Durban. Retief and his followers confiscated Sikonyela's cattle, and cheerful in their ignorance, returned to Mgundgundhlovu. With 70 Boers and their retainers, double the strength needed to break the power of the Ndebele, the Governor believed there was little reason to fear Dingane – or so it seemed.

Above: Wood engraving of Dingane's kraal at Mgundgundlovu, near modern Eshowe, the scene of the murder of Retief and his party.

Right: Dingane rose to his feet shouting 'Bulalani abathakathi' (Kill the wizards), and the warriors immediately attacked the Boer emissaries. In fact they were killed outside the royal kraal, on the execution rock Matiwane.

Left: Copy of the treaty between Retief and Dingane, dated 4 February 1838. It was found in a saddlebag near Retief's remains.

On 6 February 1838, with his customary amiability Dingane signed the treaty drafted by Retief (ironically in English), ceding all the land from the Umzimvubu River to the Thukela, and from the mountains to the sea, including Durban. But two days later, while Retief and his men were eating breakfast before their departure, Dingane allegedly screamed 'Kill the wizards', the signal for the entire party to be dragged to the hill of execution outside the kraal. There they were impaled and clubbed to death. A few hours later Dingane sent three regiments to attack the Boer families waiting below the Drakensberg Mountains for the word from Retief to enter Natal.

What followed scarred the Afrikaner nation for generations. Early on the morning of 17 February the Zulus attacked

the unsuspecting wagons laagered along the Bloukrans and Bushmans Rivers; in addition to the 70 men sent to Mgundgundhlovu, many of the men were away hunting or scouting for suitable land. In the merciless onslaught the Zulus killed 97 men and women, 185 children and about 250 Khoikhoi servants. So appalled were the returning menfolk by the savage mutilations that the village which eventually grew up in the vicinity bears the simple name Weenen ('weeping').

Not all the laagers were destroyed but the Zulus had driven off an estimated 25,000 head of cattle as well as sheep and horses. Many of the survivors were badly wounded, and scores of young children were orphaned by the massacre. However, in all, less than one-twelfth of the trekkers had perished, and the arrival of reinforcements soon gave heart to the survivors.

Above: The purpose of the traditional war dance was to overawe the tribe as much as to whip up martial ardour among the warriors.

Right: Early on the morning of 17 February 1838 a Zulu *impi* fell on parties of trekkers camped on the Bloukrans (Blaauwkrantz) and Bushmans Rivers, killing 500.

The arrival of Piet Uys and Hendrik Potgieter enabled the trekkers to field a huge commando of 350 men, although the two leaders were more inclined to quarrel with each other than to fight the Zulus at times. On 11 April they met the main Zulu force near eThaleni, but the quarrels of the Boer leaders led them to make unco-ordinated attacks. Potgieter's force was beaten off, making it impossible for him to support Uys in his so-far successful attack on the Zulus' left horn. He and his men found themselves surrounded, and tried to cut their way to freedom. Eight Boers were dragged from their horses, and Uys was mortally wounded while trying to fit a new flint to his musket. As he lay dying Uys ordered his men to save themselves. For 14-year-old Dirk Uys the thought of his father about to be speared to death was too much. He wheeled his pony and galloped back to his father, killing three warriors before falling dead across his father's corpse.

In the recriminations which followed Potgieter was blamed for the defeat of the *Vlugkommando* ('runaway commando') and in disgust he withdrew to the highveld. It was unfair, but it was a shocking reminder to the trekkers that divine protection could not compensate for tactical errors and quarrels among military leaders. The losses of the *Vlugkommando* were, however, slight, compared with the defeat suffered by the Durban settlers. All but four settlers died, along with over 600 black allies. By 24 April Zulus were on the Berea in Durban, ransacking the settlement while the frightened settlers watched from the deck of a ship in the middle of the harbour. Dreams of the *lekker lewe* in Natal seemed at an end.

THE GREAT TREK
RETRIBUTION AT BLOOD RIVER

Andries Pretorius planned his retribution against Dingane and the Zulus with great thoroughness. He reached the camp of the United Laagers late in November 1838 with 60 men and a small cannon. At once he moved out with 464 men, leaving the wagons laagered against any possible attack.

This time there was a unified command, and Pretorius was the best leader the Boers could ask for. His mounted men were to fight in the traditional manner, but he insisted on taking a wagon train, in order to have a defensible position each night. This was not to be a cattle-raid but a strategic counterstroke to break the military power of the Zulus.

The commando crossed the Thukela and Klip rivers and by Sunday 9 December they were encamped on the banks of the Waschbankspruit. Sarel Cilliers, a veteran of Vegkop and now acting as chaplain, proposed a vow or covenant: if God would grant a victory the Boers would build a church and forever afterwards celebrate the anniversary. All the Boers but five, and all the Englishmen swore the covenant.

The main Zulu force was lurking in the vicinity but patrols failed to locate it. On 15 December the commando crossed the Ncome (now known as the Blood River) and laagered overnight to keep the Sabbath. The position was exceptionally strong, with the laagered wagons on a high point on the left bank. Each *disselboom* (yoking pole) was run under the bed of the next wagon, the wheels were covered with rawhide shields and lanterns were hung from the whipstocks in case of a night attack. Draft oxen and horses were tethered inside the perimeter, and stocks of gunpowder and bullets were placed on wagon-beds and between the wheels.

Next morning at first light the early risers saw to their surprise an estimated 10-12,000 Zulu warriors sitting silently, watching the camp – in the words of one witness it looked like 'All Zululand'. The defenders rushed to their positions, the Zulus rose to their feet as one man and charged. But the strength of the position told against the Zulus. There was no room to hurl an assegai or use a knobkerrie, and warriors were trampled to death as they tried to approach the wagons above them. The defenders could hardly miss as they fired volley after volley of musketry into the seething mass of Zulus.

This phase of the battle probably lasted two hours, and a

Above: Sarel Cilliers played an heroic role at Vegkop, and with Andries Pretorius drafted the Blood River Covenant.

Right: A tinted lithograph of the Battle of Blood River, fought on 16 December 1838. The Boers defeated Dingane and avenged Retief.

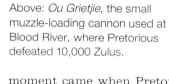

Above: *Ou Grietjie*, the small muzzle-loading cannon used at Blood River, where Pretorious defeated 10,000 Zulus.

moment came when Pretorius sensed that the Zulu attacks were weakening. Two wagons were rolled aside to allow the mounted men to pour out in a counter-attack. The Zulu regiments recoiled, losing the cohesion that was their most effective tactic. Retreat soon turned into headlong flight, and all that day parties of mounted Boers hunted down groups of fugitives. Over 3000 corpses were counted outside the laager, while Boer losses were limited to four wounded. One of these was Andries Pretorius, who sustained an assegai wound in his hand during a hand-to-hand fight with a Zulu.

The victorious commando pushed on as soon as possible to Mgundgundhlovu, but Dingane had fled northwards. The remains of Retief and his men were discovered, and on Retief's body was conveniently found the deed assigning Natal to the Boers. The *Wenkommando* (victory commando) recovered 5000 head of stolen cattle but the raiding party ran into a trap and had to retreat in the face of the surviving Zulu regiments. Their retreat was contested and when they returned to Mgundgundhlovu Pretorius ordered the whole force to retire.

Blood River was a clear-cut and decisive victory but it did not end Zulu military power. Modern critics question its true significance, but to the hard-pressed and despairing Boers it had all the attributes of divine intervention. Without firearms it would, of course, have been a different story. It was also a firmly directed battle, under one unchallenged leader who had a straightforward objective. Above all, Blood River secured the survival of the trekkers in Natal, for the moment at least.

Left: Zulus attacking a laager of
wagons. Barriers of thorn bush
made an impenetrable obstacle to
an enemy.

THE SETTLERS IN NATAL

Despite the victory at Blood River the Republic of Natalia was short-lived. A vindictive cattle-raid against the Zulus – the *Beestekommando* – threatened to destroy the fragile peace in Natal. Just as the Governor of the Cape, Napier, was trying to secure some sort of settlement news came of a further offensive against the amaBaca clan. Negotiations were broken off immediately.

To complicate matters the death of Dingane in 1841 persuaded many thousands of refugees that it was now safe to move back into their homelands. The Volksraad tried to answer complaints from Boer settlers by threatening to move the black immigrants southwards. The paramount chief of the amaMpondo complained to the British that the newcomers were being driven onto his tribal lands.

The British solution was to order the nearest troops in amaMpondoland to abandon their outpost and march on Durban. The Volksraad was stunned by the turn of events, and could only send petitions to Napier in a futile attempt to stave off annexation. When that ploy failed the Boers prepared to fight it out.

The British troops under Captain Smith built a stockade at Durban, and showed no willingness to leave, even when the Boers stole their draught oxen. Pretorius beat off a night sortie and invested the stockade, penning nearly 500 people in the small encampment. Although Smith lacked food and a good water-supply he was determined not to surrender. He asked Dick King, a 29-year-old trader to summon help from Grahamstown, 600 miles to the south. King, who had already

Left: Captain Smith occupied Port Natal in May 1842 but when his attack on the Boer camp failed he and his men were besieged.

Below left: Dick King rode to Grahamstown to bring help to Port Natal, covering the distance in ten days.

Above: Wood engraving of the British camp on the road to Umgeni, following the retreat from Congella after the defeat by Andries Pretorius.

Right: Dick King's Zulu companion Ndongeni, photographed many years after the famous Ride. He was granted a plot of land as a reward.

had many adventures during his 14 years in Natal, undertook to make the lengthy journey on horseback. Accompanied by a young Zulu retainer Ndongeni he towed two horses to Salisbury Island, saddled up and waded across the narrow channel to the mainland.

'Dick King's Ride' is part of Natal folklore. He and Ndongeni achieved in ten days what usually took over three weeks, escaping their Boer pursuers by a mixture of fieldcraft and luck. A blacksmith found them in a state of exhaustion on the racecourse at Grahamstown. It is pleasing to record that not only was King rewarded for his services but so too was Ndongeni, who was granted a piece of land outside Durban.

The arrival of the frigate HMS *Southampton* at Durban turned the tables. Her five companies of infantry were more than enough to persuade Pretorius to raise the 34-day siege. Colonel Cloete, commanding the reinforcements, took a strong line with the Volksraad, informing them that they would have to acknowledge the rule of Queen Victoria, return all captured property and hand over any wanted miscreants. Pretorius had been sustained by the mistaken belief that the Netherlands would come to his rescue, but even the highveld Boers showed little interest in Natalia's problems. The document of surrender was signed on 15 July 1842.

For a while the Volksraad continued to exercise *de facto* rule, but the conditions of near-anarchy could not last forever. After three years of bitter negotiations, minor violence and loud wrangling the decision was made to annex Natal to the Cape Colony as a district.

The infant colony was poor and unimportant, but it was given all the panoply of a segment of the British Empire. Martin West was appointed Lieutenant-Governor, and an obscure official from Fort Peddie, Theophilus Shepstone, was given a seat on the Executive Council as Diplomatic Agent to the black tribes in Natal.

For the Boers it was a bitter disappointment. All the sufferings and privations of the past decade had been wasted and the long arm of British power had stretched out to entrap them. There was no choice but to inspan the oxen once more and trek into the interior.

Top: Mpande reviewing his warriors at Ndondwengu. Dingane's half-brother allied himself with the Boers, thereby granting his people 30 years of comparative peace and prosperity.

Above: The frigate HMS *Southampton* rushed reinforcements to Port Natal to aid Captain Smith in June 1842.

THE BOER REPUBLICS

The new territory of Transorangia suffered because of the variety of people contained within its borders. In the south were Adam Kok and the Griquas, to the east were the Rolong under Moroka and the Sotho under Moshweshwe. The whites comprised trekboers under Michiel Oberholzer, who favoured British protection, and republican trekkers under Andries Potgieter.

The British Governor Sir George Napier was anxious to protect the northern borders without incurring heavy expenditure, but when he signed treaties with Adam Kok and Moshweshwe in 1843 even the loyal trekboers refused to accept black rule. In May 1845 a British force defeated a group of armed trekkers at Swartkoppies but unrest continued. In February 1848 Sir Harry Smith annexed the territory between the Drakensberg and the Vaal and Orange rivers, naming it the Orange River Sovereignty. Andries Pretorius was so provoked by this act that he led a large commando against the British in southern Transorangia. This time, however, his military skill proved insufficient and Sir Harry Smith won the Battle of Boomplaats on 29 August decisively.

Once again the Afrikaners were faced with the choice of trekking north or bending the knee to British rule. However this time events were to work against the British. Controlling the vast territory of the Orange River Sovereignty was a costly business, especially while the Colony was fighting the bloody Eighth Frontier War which lasted from 1850 to 1853. Pretorius seized his advantage, and at the Sand River Convention in January 1852 he succeeded in persuading the British finally to recognise the independence of the Transvaal trekker republic. It had taken 18 years to realise this objective of the original Voortrekkers.

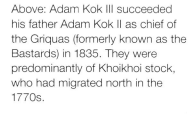

Above: Adam Kok III succeeded his father Adam Kok II as chief of the Griquas (formerly known as the Bastards) in 1835. They were predominantly of Khoikhoi stock, who had migrated north in the 1770s.

Left: Thaba Bosiu (Mountain of the Night) was chosen as an almost impregnable stronghold by Moshweshwe in 1824. It became a magnet for refugees, and out of these Moshweshwe forged the Basuto nation.

The British had secretly decided to abandon the Orange River Sovereignty but for reasons of internal politics independence was not granted until the Bloemfontein Convention in February 1854. The creation of the Orange Free State was even more significant than the Sand River Convention; for the first time the British were prepared to abandon a territory that they had previously annexed.

The fledgling republic was tiny, numbering only 12,000 white inhabitants in 1856, mostly farmers. By 1880 the capital Bloemfontein had only 2500 inhabitants of whom 1600 were white. The State President was elected for five years, citizenship was restricted to whites who had been resident for six months, and men over the age of 18 had the vote.

The Transvaal trekkers named their state the South African Republic in September 1853. Like the Orange Free State the population was largely rural, approximately 15,000 whites and an estimated 100,000 blacks in 1852; by the 1880s the population had risen to 43,000 whites and over 700,000 blacks.

Citizenship and the vote were reserved exclusively for whites. To ensure an abundance of black manpower two categories of labour were created, ordinary workers and indentured labourers. The latter were orphaned black children, and bound to their masters until the age of 25. It was a system that lent itself to abuse, despite regulations to control any obvious irregularities.

Above: Wood engraving of Moshweshwe, a statesman and strategist, in 1833. He created the Basuto people and gave them stability, enabling them to absorb and civilize cannibals and bandits.

Right: The scene after the skirmish at Swartkoppies (Zwartkopjes) in May 1845, in which mounted Dragoon Guards defeated a Boer force.

Above right: The capture of Fort Armstrong during the Eighth Frontier War. Forces included the Royal Artillery, Cape Mounted Rifles, burghers from Beaufort and Fingo levies.

Left: Colonel Sir Harry Smith pursuing Hintsa during the Sixth Frontier War (1834-35). As Governor and High Commissioner he also brought the 'War of the Axe' to an end.

Right: A conference at Block Drift between Colonel John Hare and Sandile. It failed to avert the Seventh Frontier War – the 'War of the Axe' – during which the Xhosa defeated Hare.

The Free State soon earned an enviable reputation under President Brand as a model of stability, whereas the Transvaal was plagued by internal wrangling. The death of Potgieter in 1852 and Pretorius the following year robbed the Republic of experienced leadership, and it was to be some years before the quarrelsome white communities accepted one constitution, one Volksraad and one flag.

The worst moment for the new republic came only a year after unification. Both the son of Andries Pretorius and Potgieter's successor Stephanus Schoeman were determined to rule, and when Martinus Wessel Pretorius was forced to relinquish the office of President in 1860 Schoeman supporters in Potchefstroom marched on Pretoria and proclaimed their leader Acting State President. The civil war which ensued did not die down until 1864, when Paul Kruger inflicted a final defeat on the rebels, enabling M W Pretorius to play the peacemaker between the groups.

Above: Bloemfontein in 1852. It was the main centre of population in the Orange Free State, although in number of inhabitants it was quite small.

Right: Martinus Wessel Pretorious, the son of Andries Pretorius was elected President of the Transvaal in 1857. He tried to unite the two Boer republics and was elected President of the Orange Free State in 1859.

INDIAN IMMIGRATION

Although in terms of historical accuracy the first Indians went to the Cape of Good Hope as freed slaves in the seventeenth century, the first immigration as such did not start until 1860. Indentured labour was imported into Natal to work on the new sugar plantations, and within six years over 6000 men and women had landed at Durban.

The terms of indenture allowed for five years' work. At the end of five years a labourer could sign on for another five years, or be released, or return to India at his own expense. Those who signed for the full ten years were entitled to a free passage back to India.

The recruits for the sugar plantations came mainly from Madras; 80 per cent were Hindus, some 12 per cent Muslims and the remainder Christian or pagan. The contribution they made to the prosperity of Natal was immense. The small colony was not rich, but sugar exports helped to push general revenue up by over 3000 percent in 30 years.

Sadly the first Indians to be repatriated in 1871 reported that they had not been well treated, citing instances of flogging and pay-stoppages for illness. The Indian Government stopped further recruiting until specific reforms were implemented, but immigration was restarted in 1874.

The Indian community in Natal flourished. By 1880 the population had grown to nearly 12,000, and a new class of 'passenger' Indians came into existence, mainly Gujerati Muslims who came as traders rather than as labourers. Their entrepreneurial skill was to bring them into conflict with white traders who resented undercutting, and black customers who

Top: Indian labourers arriving at Durban to begin their five-year indentures.

Above: Indian labourers cutting sugar cane. Recruits came mainly from Madras and were better able to survive the heat and arduous working conditions.

Left: The Indian Market in Durban. The newcomers flourished and by 1880 the Indian population in Natal had grown to 12,000.

Grey Street — Durban

Indian Temple (Mosque) — Durban

resented what was seen as usurious trading on credit.

The role of the Indians was thus bound to cause problems. Their efficiency and flair for business merely increased their unpopularity. Attempts to establish Indian businesses in the Transvaal were met with restrictions on residential and trading rights; Natal imposed a £3 tax on Indians who wished to stay in the colony after the expiry of their indentures.

In the years after the Anglo-Boer War Indian political aspirations became more articulate. A young lawyer, M K Gandhi, had played a leading role in setting up the Natal Indian Congress as long ago as 1894, and after 1902 he took up the cause of Indians in the Transvaal. Using the methods of passive resistance, *Satyagraha*, Gandhi was able to embarrass the Government. When more than 2000 *satyagrahis* marched into the Transvaal in 1913 the authorities could do little beyond making mass arrests. Thousands of supporters were willing to go to gaol, thereby seriously threatening work on the sugar estates. Gandhi's imprisonment only increased the South African Government's problems; although London was unwilling to meddle in the new Union's affairs, the British authorities were under pressure from India to do something to protect Indians in South Africa.

Jan Smuts, the Minister for the Interior, was under considerable pressure to conciliate the Indians, and an Indian Inquiry Commission was appointed. The resulting Indian Relief Act of 1914 went some way to removing the disabilities, notably the £3 tax on time-expired labourers and the refusal to recognise the validity of Indian marriages. Gandhi left South Africa convinced that he had liberated his countrymen. In fact they were still denied political representation and it was still not permissible for Indians to reside anywhere in the Orange Free State.

Post-war the pressure was renewed for political representation. At the 1921 Imperial Conference Indians claimed citizenship on the grounds that they were part of the British Empire, but Smuts rejected the claim. When the subject came up again two years later, the South African Indian Congress was formed to provide a forum for discontent.

The collapse of the post-war boom put an end to any hope of major reform for the Indians and other blacks. The white working class had its back to the wall, and there was little sympathy to spare. It was a depressing portent for the future of the states.

Left: Mahatma Gandhi as a young Durban barrister. He played a leading part in campaigning for Indian rights in Natal and the Transvaal.

Below: The figure of 'Sammy'. The itinerant Indian trader rapidly became part of South African folklore.

Above left: Grey Street, Durban, with Indian pedestrians.

Left: A Durban mosque. The majority of early immigrants were Madrasi Hindus, but later arrivals were mainly Gujerati Muslims.

Right: Durban from the Berea in 1873. Although the port handled a lucrative trade the colony's finances were precarious.

THE DIAMOND FIELDS

The future of South Africa changed forever when two children discovered a diamond at Hopetown on the Orange River in 1867. The diamond fields lay in territory that had been bought by M W Pretorius from Adam Kok in 1861, but rival claims were presented by the South African Republic, the Griquas, the Rolong and the Thlapin. The dispute was settled by arbitration under the aegis of the Governor of Natal. The so-called 'Keate Award' made by the Lieutenant-Governor of Natal came down on the side of the Griquas' claims, but Nikolaas Waterboer offered the territory (designated Griqualand West) to the Crown. To add a further twist, in 1876 the Land Court declared Waterboer's claim invalid, and the Crown paid £90,000 to the Orange Free State as compensation.

Once the significance of the Hopetown discovery was understood the Diamond Rush began, with prospectors heading for the alluvial diggings at Pniel and Klipdrift (later renamed Barkly West) and later for the 'dry' diggings at Dutoitspan and Bultfontein. By the middle of 1871 the 'Big Hole' at Kimberley gave promise of unimagined wealth – the four great volcanic 'pipes' yielded over £60 million in the first ten years.

The early days of the diamond fields were anarchic, much as they had been in America in the 1849 Gold Rush and later in the Australian Gold Rush. Diggers' Committees sprang up, even a Diggers' Republic at Klipdrift, representing an estimated 40,000 miners at various times. But the long-term future of the diamond fields could only be assured by stable government and sound industrial management. Annexation by the Cape in 1871 followed the granting of colonial status to Griqualand West.

In 1874 Cecil Rhodes and his associates floated the De Beers Company to buy up and consolidate small claims. The Cape

Left: Nikolaas Waterboer was the son of Andries Waterboer, declared paramount chief of the Griquas in 1822. His claim to the Klipdrift diamond diggings was upheld but later invalidated.

Right: The Kimberley Mine in 1877. The 'Big Hole' had already obliterated Coleberg Kopje, and would yield over £60 million by 1881.

Top: The first diamond diggings on the Vaal River at Klipdrift. 'No houses were erected, all lived in tents, and took the diamond ground down to the river to wash and sort on the tables on the banks . . . '

Left: Harsh measures were taken to prevent black mineworkers from stealing diamonds.

Above: A wood-and-iron store at Du Toit's Pan, c1871. The flag with the horse on a red background quartered by the Union Flag may represent the 'Diggers' Republic' of Stafford Parker, which lasted from 1870 to 1871.

Colony was a channel for supplying European capital as well as significant amounts of local capital for developing the fields. Suddenly the Colony found itself transformed from a debtor to a creditor. The insatiable demands of the diamond fields generated greater shipping activity, and railways began to replace the time-honoured ox-wagons.

Meanwhile Rhodes consolidated his hold on the diamond mining industry. He saw correctly that deep mining called for one large company capable of mining an entire 'pipe' economically and safely. In collaboration with Alfred Beit and the rival *Compagnie Française* Rhodes and his New De Beers Company (floated in 1880) began a long battle to buy out the Kimberley Central Company. This titanic struggle was finally won in 1889, leaving Rhodes and his De Beers Consolidated Company in undisputed control.

Left: Johannes Nicolaas de Beer, one of the brothers who owned the Vooruitzigt farm on which diamonds were discovered.

Below: Black mineworkers of the Grahamstown Gold Mining Company, which despite its name was mining gold in the Transvaal.

The effect of the Diamond Rush on the various black communities was catastrophic. At first tribes like the Sotho prospered by supplying grain and cattle to feed the mushrooming communities in the diamond fields, but in the longer term it was labour that the diamond mines needed.

As the mines sucked in ever-growing numbers of migrant labourers it became necessary to control the migrants. Many black workers took a rifle in lieu of wages and then decamped to their home villages. Others smuggled uncut diamonds, to sell them outside the diamond fields. To put a stop to these practices a compound system was set up, providing accommodation and food, but at a cost of severely restricted freedom for the duration of the work-contract. What emerged was a permanent class of unskilled black labour, in sharp contrast to the pool of professional white miners.

Having achieved the wealth that he craved Cecil Rhodes turned his attention to politics, becoming MP for Barkley West in 1881. When he became Premier of the Cape Colony in 1890 he tried to impose his vision of an Imperial future on the rest of South Africa. Although credited by many, particularly Afrikaners in the two independent republics, with some sinister collusion with the British Government, the records show that Rhodes preferred to act without London's approval. He despised the slow, timid and often contradictory policies of governments, and hoped to achieve his dream of a British South Africa without London's help. Paradoxically it was with the help of the Cape Afrikaner Bond that his political ambitions were realised. Both Rhodes and J H Hofmeyr, leader of the Afrikaner Bond, wanted a prosperous, powerful and independent Cape Colony. Hofmeyr had no wish to divide the white population and saw the potential disaster of a war with Great Britain, but he can have had little idea of where Rhodes's overweening ambition would lead him.

Above: Coat of arms of the *Afrikansche Bond*, the first major Afrikaner political organization. First proposed by the Rev. S J du Toit in 1879, its first branch was formed a year later.

Above left: Washing gear at the Bultfontein diamond mine, one of the first 'dry diggings' opened in 1870. The 'blue ground' had to be crushed and washed to allow the diamonds to be recovered.

Left: A Kimberley compound, c1900. Black workers were given accommodation and food but had their freedom severely restricted.

Right: Cecil Rhodes, Premier of the Cape Colony, and his ministers.

PART II
ESTABLISHING THE REPUBLICS

BRITAIN ANNEXES THE TRANSVAAL

From the start the South African Republic was hamstrung by being landlocked. All imported goods came northwards from the Cape, through Natal or through Mozambique. M W Pretorius tried to define the Transvaal's boundaries in 1868, with a narrow corridor giving access to the coast, but both the Portuguese and the British took such a strong stand that the claim was never put to the test.

The death of Pretorius in 1871 left a vacuum in Transvaal politics, and after an attempt to get President Brand of the Orange Free State to accept the Presidency, it went to Thomas François Burgers, a clergyman. Although hampered by chronic financial difficulties Burgers tackled the problems with some vigour. The foundations were laid for a permanent military force, education was expanded and diplomatic links were established with European countries. To foster independence from the British colonies, good relations were encouraged with the Portuguese in Mozambique, with a view to using Delagoa Bay as a lifeline to the outside world.

Burgers was soon in deep trouble, however. An over-ambitious scheme to build a rail link to Delagoa Bay collapsed, and

Right: British troops bringing Sekhukhuni into Pretoria in November 1879. The Pedi chieftain was released in 1881 but was murdered a year later by his half-brother.

Below: President Thomas François Burgers. The 38-year-old clergyman was sworn in at Pretoria in 1872, and worked hard, but he could not prevent British annexation.

a campaign against the dissident Pedi chieftain Sekhukhuni was bungled. Many farmers in the eastern Transvaal began to doubt the ability of the Government to protect them from raids, and appeals were made by the gold-mining communites to the British to help them.

For the British it was an opportunity to promote their ideal of a federation of their colonies and the Boer republics. The British Foreign Secretary Lord Carnarvon put the idea to Burgers, but in spite of the President's understandable reluctance he pushed ahead. In theory annexation was all that was necessary; the Free State would be unable to sustain its existence outside the new federation.

The instrument of federation was Sir Theophilus Shepstone, Natal's Secretary for Native Affairs. Armed with an unsigned commission from Carnarvon and imprecise instructions, Shepstone went to Pretoria to proceed with annexation, provided that he had the consent of the (white) population. It was a fatal blunder, for Shepstone had no experience of dealing with Afrikaners, and even less awareness of the complexities involved in running the South African Republic. His attempts to force President Burgers to institute reforms failed; the Volksraad remained defiant, taking its cue from the newly-elected Vice-President Paul Kruger. On 12 April 1877 the Union Jack was hoisted in Pretoria, and the South African Republic passed under British control.

At first annexation seemed popular but Afrikaners in the Cape and the Free State were dismayed by the turn of events. All hope of confederation vanished in a wave of protest. Nor

Above: Sekhukhuni after his capture. Troops commanded by Sir Garnet Wolseley, assisted by 8000 Swazi warriors forced the Pedi to surrender and brought a humiliating rebellion to an end.

Left: The capture of Sekhukhuni's stronghold. An attempt by Boer commandos had failed through cowardice and it was considered essential to bring the Pedi to heel to ensure the safety of the Transvaal.

Pages 58-59: *The last man of the family to leave* by E J Austen.

The Transvaal.—South African Republic. Annexation, 1877: Retrocession, 1881.

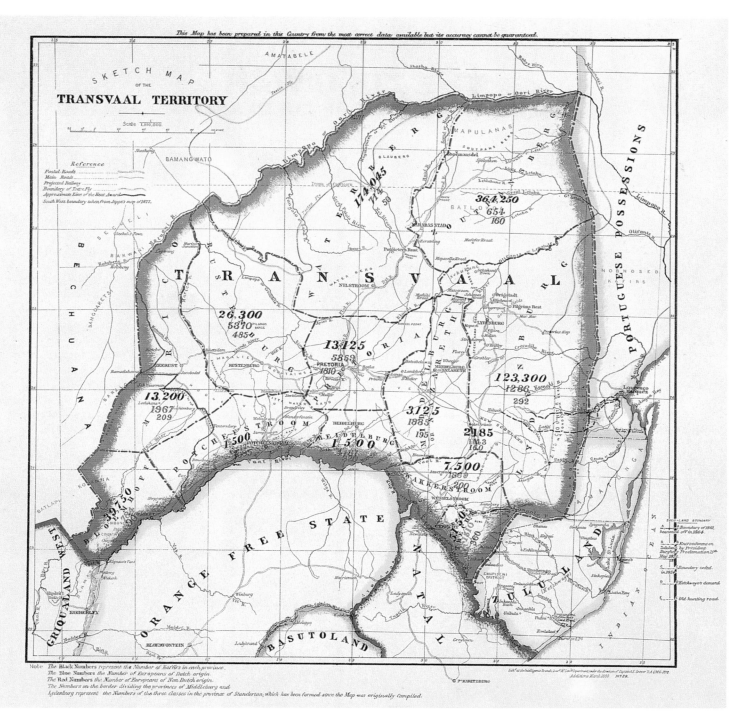

Above: Sketch map of the Transvaal in 1878, showing the distribution of the population by race.

Left: Portraits of the leading figures involved in the 1877 annexation and the 1881 retrocession of the Transvaal, published in the *Cape Argus* in August 1881.

Right: Henry Howard Molyneux Herbert, fourth Earl of Carnarvon and twice Colonial Secretary.

was Shepstone any more enlightened during his term in office than the unfortunate ex-President Burgers. Financial control was poor and Shepstone's autocratic manner soon alienated sympathy among the Afrikaners. Paul Kruger had little difficulty in rallying support against the new rulers who had run up large debts and had abandoned the Delagoa Bay Railway once more. Sekhukhuni refused to pay the fine levied on him by the Burgers Government, and Shepstone had too few troops to enforce collection. He also failed to keep the Zulus in check on the south-eastern border, with the result that local farmers began to abandon their land.

The recall of Shepstone in 1879 did little to restore confidence in British rule, but by the end of the year Sir Garnet Wolseley succeeded in capturing Sekhukhuni, having also defeated the Zulus. These events came too late, however, to deflect the Transvaalers from their determination to rid themselves of British rule. Their determination would bring about yet another collision with the British, but this time the Boers would win the day.

THE ZULU WAR
THE INVASION OF ZULULAND

The death of Mpande in 1872 tempted Sir Theophilus Shepstone to extend British influence beyond the northern frontier of Natal. Mpande's heir, Cetshwayo, had continuing problems with the Transvaal Boers, and looked to Natal for redress. In the autumn of 1873 Shepstone induced Cetshwayo to take part in a 'coronation' of dubious legality, and it looked as if *Somtseu* ('Great Hunter' as the Zulus nicknamed Shepstone) would champion the Zulus. But after the annexation of the Transvaal Shepstone began to see them as a threat to his grand design for British influence over the region.

Shepstone behaved in a high-handed manner towards Cetshwayo and was determined to use military force to crush him. A boundary commission had rejected claims of the Boers, but Shepstone informed the Zulus that the Boers were to be left in possession. An ultimatum was presented to the Zulu king, virtually demanding a total surrender of authority, and when no suitable reply was achieved the military commander, Lieutenant-General Lord Chelmsford, was ordered to invade Zululand on 11 January 1879.

British hopes of a speedy victory were dashed when Chelmsford's Central Column was destroyed by a huge Zulu *impi* at Isandhlwana. Cetshwayo's half-brother Dabulamanzi had strict orders not to cross into Natal, but flushed by victory his warriors attacked the small British outpost at Rorke's Drift. The British troops defended the position gallantly, defeating 3-4000 Zulus and earning 11 Victoria Crosses as a result. Nevertheless the news of Isandhlwana threw the Natal colonists into a panic, and nothing less than the destruction of the Zulus would satisfy them. The British Army too, needed a convincing victory over the Zulus to wipe out the stain of the defeat of Isandhlwana.

The Zulu Army had done much better than anyone could

Above: Lieutenants Coghill and Melville died trying to save the Colours of the 24th Regiment after the disaster at Isandhlwana. The Colours were never found.

Right: Dabulamanzi was half-brother to Cetshwayo and led the *impi* which attacked Rorke's Drift.

Far left: Cetshwayo, former King of the Zulus, in exile in Cape Town in 1880.

Left: Lieutenant General Thesiger (later Lord Chelmsford) had considerable experience of African campaigning, having fought in the Perie Bush. He was unfairly blamed for Isandhlwana, when his subordinates tried to defend too large a perimeter with insufficient troops.

have foretold. Although the Battle of Isandhlwana took a heavy toll of lives — Cetshwayo said, 'An assegai has been plunged into the belly of the nation' when he heard of the losses — his warriors immobilised Colonel Pearson's Right Flank Column at Eshowe by running off the troops' draught oxen. The Left Flank Column under Sir Evelyn Wood was also forced to entrench at Kambula, and the invasion of Zululand was temporarily at an end.

Following pages: The final moments of the British defeat at Isandhlwana as painted by M E Newman.

Reinforcements were rushed out to Natal, and by April Chelmsford was able to relieve Eshowe. Wood's force inflicted a sharp defeat at Kambula, showing that brave men with assegais could not match breech-loading rifles. To set against their heroic victory at Isandhlwana the Zulus had suffered at least 6000 dead, and still the English were pouring into the Zulu kingdom.

It has been fashionable to blame Chelmsford for the initial disaster but the records show that his subordinates committed a series of small blunders. By themselves none would have caused the destruction of the camp, but in the face of Zulu tactical skill and the almost unbelievable bravery of the young warriors the sum total of the mistakes was to prove disastrous. The main error was to disperse the defenders around too large a perimeter; at a crucial moment during the firefight some troops started to run out of ready-use ammunition, and before reserves could be rushed to the troops the Zulus had punched a hole in the line. Of the 1000 Imperial troops in camp over 600 and another 60 Europeans died; some 600 of the black auxiliary troops, drivers and servants were also killed.

The heroism of the defenders of Rorke's Drift should not obscure the deeds of the Zulu attackers. Dabulamanzi's men had already fought at Isandhlwana for six hours, where they suffered heavy casualties. Despite having outstripped their supplies for several days previously they were still able to cross the flooded Buffalo River and start another attack on the post at Rorke's Drift within two hours. The attacks continued through the night, and it can only have been the Zulus' sheer exhaustion that saved the tiny garrison.

For the Zulus it was a tragic miscalculation. Young men, unaware of the massed rifle-fire they would face, and brought up on the achievements of Shaka and of their forefathers, had talked of 'washing their spears'. The glories of the past had bred an arrogance and pride which made the regiments hard to control, and Cetshwayo was ill-equipped to cope with pressure from European imperialism.

Above left: Engraving of sailors of the Naval Brigade crossing the Tukhela River on their way to relieve Eshowe.

Left: The men who won 11 VCs at Rorke's Drift; the 2/24th Regiment pose for a group photograph on 22 January 1879.

Above: Sir Evelyn Wood's troops repulse an attack on the entrenched camp at Kambula Hill, 29 March 1879.

Right: Zulu indunas, two wearing the *isicoco* (head ring).

THE ZULU WAR
THE OVERTHROW OF ZULU MILITARY POWER

When his reinforcements reached him Chelmsford was able to start the second invasion of Zululand in May 1879, but this time it was to be a methodical advance, with none of the over-confidence of before. It was too much to expect that the general would retain the confidence of the public and the British Government, but the British Government chose a compromise which put Chelmsford in a particularly invidious position. He was left with his rank and position unchanged, but General Sir Garnet Wolseley was appointed as Governor of Natal and High Commissioner for 'Native and Foreign Affairs to the Northward and Eastward of these Colonies'.

The appointment came too late to stop Chelmsford's progress. With his flanking columns secure and about 16,000 Imperial and colonial troops (to say nothing of 7000 armed Natal native troops) his only problem was a chronic shortage of oxen and wagons. By the end of May the lumbering columns had reached the Blood River and were poised for the blow against Ulundi, the royal kraal. The Zulu Army was still at large, battered but dangerous, and Chelmsford knew that an attack on Cetshwayo's 'capital' was the only way to bring the regiments to battle.

Above left: Sir Garnet Wolseley arrived in Zululand too late to claim credit for the victory at Ulundi.

Above: Cetshwayo proved very different from the bloodthirsty tyrant depicted in the South African and English press.

Left: A corporal of the 17th Lancers attends to a wound on his horse's foreleg during the Battle of Ulundi.

Above: Lancers pursuing Zulus at Ulundi.

Left: Engraving of the moment of victory at Ulundi. The last Zulu attack has been beaten off, and the four-deep square opens out to allow cavalry and mounted infantry to pursue the beaten enemy.

It was at this stage that Chelmsford suffered a further setback which almost equalled Isandhlwana in its political impact. The Prince Imperial, the only son of the former Emperor of France Napoleon III, had been living in England in exile with his mother the Empress Eugenie. As the only credible candidate for the French throne, young Louis was a focus of attention for French monarchists, and he enlisted in the British Army as an officer-cadet, winning a commission in the Royal Artillery in 1875.

In 1879 the Prince Imperial was only 22, and it was natural that he should want to go out to the Zulu War. Military experience would add some lustre to his claim to the throne, and he could hardly refuse service when his fellow-officers were being selected to go out to South Africa. So, in spite of misgivings the young ardent Frenchman was allowed to go out in a private capacity as a 'spectator'.

Above: Lieutenant Carey commanded the escort which abandoned the Prince Imperial to his fate.

Right: Embarking the remains of the Prince Imperial on board the tug *Adonis* for transfer to HMS *Boadicea* beyond the bar.

Below right: The Prince Imperial was the only son of the ex-Emperor Napoleon III and the Empress Eugénie. He lived with his mother in exile in England.

On the fatal day the Prince had been ordered to make sketches of the route to the column's next campsite. That afternoon his escort, under the command of Lieutenant Carey, was ambushed while resting at a small, apparently deserted kraal. In the panic the troopers saddled up and rode for their lives, but the Prince's horse shied, preventing him from mounting. Alone and armed only with a revolver Louis was quickly killed by the Zulu assegais. By the time Carey could rally the four survivors of the escort it was obvious that he was outnumbered, and he had no choice but to ride back to the main camp.

The death of a princeling, even a French one, was all that the press needed, and the unheroic circumstances of his death made matters worse. The conduct of Carey cast a slur on the rest of the Army, and his undignified attempts to justify his conduct merely made matters worse.

Disregarding a flood of peremptory telegrams from Wolseley, Chelmsford reached Ulundi on 3 July, ready for battle the next day. The result was a foregone conclusion. The four-deep square had sufficient firepower to inflict terrible losses on the Zulus, and none got within 30 yards of the line. The only Imperial casualties suffered were from stray bullets fired into the mass of men, horses and cattle. When the last rushes had spent themselves, the cavalry and mounted infantry emerged from the square to drive the Zulus from the field.

The destruction of Ulundi was effectively the end of the war, although Cetshwayo was not captured for another two months. Wolseley divided Zululand into 13 small kingdoms, a solution that pleased no one. Finally in 1887 the British annexed the country in a vain attempt to bring the anarchy and discontent to an end. Even so, it took another ten years before peace settled over Zululand, and in 1897 it was finally possible to incorporate Tongaland and Zululand in Natal.

The Zulu Empire had lasted scarcely 60 years, during which time millions of people had been killed or driven from their tribal lands. But, for all the destruction and bloodshed, the achievements of the House of Shaka remain unique in South African history.

PAUL KRUGER

Paul Kruger's life spanned the Battle of Blood River to the end of the South African Republic. As he liked to remind his audiences, he had seen the circle of wagons, the children melting lead to make bullets, and the women hacking off the arms of those Zulus who tried to break through the thorn bush between the wagons. With his baggy black suit and his huge pipe the old man personified the Republic's idea of the rural 'backveld' Boer.

To the British, particularly the fastidious Alfred Milner and Joseph Chamberlain, Kruger was an 'ignorant, dirty, cunning old man', but both critics underrated Kruger's complexities and undoubted political skills. Born in 1825 in the Cape Colony to a trekboer family of German origin, young Paul and his family had joined Andries Potgieter on the Great Trek. His formal education was nil, but his father read the Bible aloud at table. His profession was lion-hunter but on commando he also showed his mettle. At 17 he was appointed deputy field cornet and in this capacity helped to subdue various African chiefs. At 26 he was elected as a delegate to the Sand River Convention, and within ten years he was appointed Commandant-General.

In 1877, when Great Britain annexed the Transvaal, Kruger emerged as the Boers' national champion, and was twice sent to London to try to persuade the British to abandon their policy. His prestige was greatly increased by the First Anglo-Boer War in 1881, not merely by the victory at Majuba, but by his skilful negotiations with Gladstone. In 1883 he was elected President of the South African Republic, an office he was to hold for four terms.

His mixture of animal strength and human cunning, coupled with self-reliance and faith in God, made Paul Kruger a forceful personality, but both Afrikaner and British opponents found him headstrong and autocratic. If he found him-

Above: Paul Kruger, the young lion-hunter.

Above: President Kruger in later life.

Left: President Kruger prided himself on being accessible to all citizens. Visitors were received on the verandah, where they could air the most trivial grievances over a cup of coffee.

self losing an argument he was apt to run around the room roaring; then he would resort to Biblical quotations and this would be followed by weeping, before he finally begged his opponent to give in. Other reports, however, praised his legendary patience and willingness to comprise.

His opponents in the Volksraad were led by General Piet Joubert, who accused the old man of autocratic and old-fashioned ways. The discovery of gold on the Witwatersrand in 1886 brought the Republic sudden wealth, and the policy of granting concessions undoubtedly led to corruption.

By 1893 it looked as if 'Krugerism' was nearing its end; General Joubert had polled nearly 47 per cent of the vote during the presidential election. In fairness, however, Kruger's policies did succeed in ensuring that the Transvaal and the farming community extracted the maximum benefit from the gold mining industry, so helping to put the Republic's finances on a sound footing.

Any weakness in Kruger's position was eliminated by the Jameson Raid in 1895. At a stroke the Afrikaners were united, especially the Free Staters. In 1897 President Marthinus Steyn signed a military pact with 'Oom Paul', as Kruger was affectionately known, a brilliant coup for the old man.

When the war started to go badly it was Kruger who preached a simple message to the *volk*: they should remember they were 'God's Chosen People', and if they were worthy of the Lord's intervention they would eventually triumph. Unlike Steyn, Kruger never placed any faith in foreign intervention. However he was to give way to despair after the fall of Pretoria in June 1900. He was smuggled out of the capital and went by train to Machadodorp.

The President and his staff were able to keep up appearances for a further three months, but with three large British formations pursuing them the game was soon up. Once across the Portuguese border the fugitive President was allowed to travel to Mozambique, where the Dutch cruiser *Gelderland* was waiting to take him to exile in the Netherlands. Two years later, in 1904, the ex-President died in Switzerland.

It was Paul Kruger's misfortune to lead his beloved South African Republic to defeat, but that cannot offset his stature as a leader. His political skill was greater than that of any of his Afrikaner contemporaries, with the possible exception of Marthinus Steyn, but the forces ranged against the two presidents were simply too powerful.

Above: A caricature of Paul Kruger by 'Drawl' in *Vanity Fair* in March 1900.

Left: Pencil drawing of President Kruger's house in Pretoria.

THE FIRST ANGLO-BOER WAR
THE CAUSES OF THE CONFLICT

The annexation of the Transvaal in 1877 proved extremely un-popular. Before annexation had taken effect a delegation was sent to London in an attempt to persuade Lord Carnarvon to reverse the decision. Another was sent in 1878, to put the case to Carnarvon's successor, Sir Michael Hicks Beach, but again without success.

So far, protest had been peaceful, but it was becoming clear to the Transvaalers that no one was listening. Even the return of Gladstone and the Liberals to office in April 1880 produced no shift in opinion; the new Prime Minister had changed his mind about the injustice of annexation.

Support for the Transvaal became more vocal in the Cape and the Free State, stiffening the Transvaalers' will to resist. In November 1880 an attempt to collect arrears of taxes from a farmer of Potchefstroom met with armed resistance. In December a National Committee meeting at Paardekraal was attended by over 8000 men, and preparations for war began. A triumvirate, comprising Paul Kruger, Piet Joubert and Mar-thinus Pretorius, was set up, and its first act, the following day, was to declare the restoration of the Republic. On 16 December the *Vierkleur* flag was hoisted at Heidelberg.

The obtuse Governor, Colonel Owen Lanyon, had at first convinced himself that the Boers would not fight, and as a re-

Below: Proclaiming martial law in Pretoria in December 1880, two days after Anstruther's defeat at Bronkhorstspruit.

Right: Photograph of Sir Michael Hicks Beach who succeeded the Earl of Carnarvon as Colonial Secretary after annexation.

Right: This composite photograph of the Boer leaders in 1880-81 includes Piet Joubert (second row) and other notables.

Above: The Convent Redoubt was one of several strongpoints fortified to defend Pretoria.

Right: Colonel Sir Owen Lanyon, Governor of the Transvaal, refused to believe that war would break out.

Below: The Pretoria Rifles was a volunteer regiment recruited mainly from British civilians in Pretoria.

sult his garrison was scattered about the country in small detachments. On 14 December he ordered two companies of infantry to Potchefstroom to collect tax arrears. Two days later Piet Cronje and a commando retaliated by firing on the British in their small redoubt, and the surrender of this detachment was the signal for action against the other garrisons.

On 20 December the British suffered their first major disaster, at Bronkhorstspruit, when the 94th Foot, marching in column from Lydenburg to Pretoria, were confronted by a party of 200 Boers. Lieutenant-Colonel Anstruther was told by Commandant Frans Joubert that the country was now a republic, and that any further advance would be an act of war. When Anstruther refused to turn back the Boers opened fire at a range of 200 yards. Within 15 minutes the 94th Foot had suffered the loss of 57 killed and nearly 100 wounded, and the dying Anstruther had to give the order to surrender.

The Boers now had some 7000 burghers under arms, sufficient to pin down all the surviving garrisons and to allow Piet Joubert to move to the Natal border where he planned to block any move to send reinforcements from Natal. Lanyon himself,

Left: Typical Boers as seen by the
Graphic in May 1881. The civilian
dress fostered the illusion of a
'rabble of farmers'.

still unable to explain 'what can have so suddenly caused the Boers to act as they have', was now besieged in Pretoria. He had some 1700 troops, including irregulars, and two guns, but his failure to concentrate his forces meant that the nearest detachments were nearly all over 100 miles away.

The sieges were desultory and uneventful, causing the besieged only discomfort and sickness. Conditions in the small redoubts were cramped; the redoubt at Potchefstroom was only 30 yards square. Although the Boers bottled up the British, these small sieges did in fact tie down their own limited manpower to some extent. Assaults, with the risk of heavy casualties, were not part of Boer tactics; instead, the Boers were content to wait until the defenders surrendered through lack of food or water. The war would therefore be decided by the success of the Natal garrison in forcing the mountain passes on the frontier.

THE FIRST ANGLO-BOER WAR
VICTORY AT MAJUBA

The man on whom all British hopes now rested was 45-year-old Major-General Sir George Pomeroy-Colley, commander of the hastily created Natal Field Force. With a scratch force of some 1200 troops he would have to fight his way through, at most, 7000 Boers in order to relieve the 2000-strong Transvaal garrisons.

By the last week in January 1881 the Field Force was ready to march to Mount Prospect, three miles from the frontier. But his attempt to dislodge the Boers from their entrenchments at Laing's Nek was badly co-ordinated and ended in failure.

Elated by their success, Commandant Nicolas Smit and 300 burghers then went to raid the road between Mount Prospect and Newcastle. When Colley heard that a mail convoy had been ambushed he took an Imperial battalion, four guns and a small detachment of mounted infantry to the Ingogo River crossing. Caught in a poor position, the British proved no match for the Boers in marksmanship, and only by good luck was the small force withdrawn under cover of darkness, having suffered severely.

The Natal Field Force had 340 casualties out of a strength of 1200, and Colley's position was weaker than ever. To add to his worries he learned that the British Government was negotiating with President Kruger to reverse annexation. When reinforcements arrived he was therefore tempted to wipe out the disgrace of Laing's Nek and the Ingogo by securing a convincing victory over the Boers who had invaded Natal. The

Above: Sir George Pomeroy-Colley's failure to understand his Boer opponents cost him his life at Majuba.

Left: In *Floreat Etona* Lady Butler recorded the gallant deaths of two subalterns at Laing's Nek.

towering flat-topped mountain Majuba, the 'hill of doves', dominated the area. It had not been occupied by the Boers, and Colley proposed to garrison it in a daring night march.

The operation went well, and Colley's force now overlooked all the Boer positions, including their laagers at the rear. But without artillery and armed with Martini-Henry rifles which were effective to only 400 yards, the five infantry companies could do little. To make matters worse, no attempt was made to fortify the position. When the Boers finally realised that the mountain was in British hands there was some talk of retreating, but when it became clear that there was no artillery on Majuba the bolder spirits decided to make an assault.

While some Boers gave covering fire against those British holding the saucer-shaped rim on the mountain top, others split into two groups to climb the north-east face. Commandant Joubert also cut off Colley's retreat by sending a force to the rear of Majuba. By 0700 hours roughly 300 Boers were in action, keeping up a constant fire.

At first little damage was done to the defenders beyond forcing them to keep their heads down, but by 1100 casualties were mounting. The Boers seized a knoll on the north-west side of the hill, driving the defenders back to the central position. As the battle became more confused Colley seemed to lose control completely. During the panic-stricken withdrawal that followed Colley was shot through the head, apparently as he was trying to rally the broken troops.

There was no disguising the magnitude of the Boer victory. Out of 365 British on Majuba that morning 285 were dead or wounded, at a cost of only two Boer dead and four wounded. The war was virtually over, for the British Government had no option but to allow Sir Evelyn Wood to arrange a truce. His provisional peace terms, negotiated on 6 March, were ratified by the Convention of Pretoria.

Under the terms of the Convention, the Transvaal won back

its independence at the cost of accepting British suzerainty, a British Resident to oversee African affairs, British control over the eastern border native districts and British approval of the republic's foreign affairs. Even these conditions were temporary, and the 1884 Convention of London removed the provisions for suzerainty and the British Resident. The British had suffered a major military and political defeat.

All in all Majuba was a mighty victory. It marked a new stage in the creation of an assertive, unified Afrikaner nationalism. It also inflicted a wound to British pride sufficiently deep to make the Second Anglo-Boer War an inevitable consequence. In military terms, notwithstanding the many lessons it had for contemporary British leadership and infantry tactics, it was no more than a skirmish. The numbers involved on both sides were insignificant, out of all proportion to its strategic consequences. Today Majuba is remembered chiefly as the day when David toppled Goliath, and seen as another example of divine protection for the *volk*.

Above: Majuba, 'the hill of doves', dominated Colley's only route to the Transvaal.

Left: Armistice negotiations between Sir Evelyn Wood VC (seated, right) and Piet Joubert (centre left), 9 March 1881.

Above left: Men of the 94th Regiment and volunteers guarding grazing draught oxen.

Right: Boer and British signatories to the armistice pose for a photograph. The ceasefire was ratified by the Convention of Pretoria.

THE DISCOVERY OF GOLD

The first 'gold fever' hit the Transvaal in the 1870s, first near Pietersburg and then in the eastern Transvaal, at Pilgrim's Rest, Lydenburg and De Kaap. Even so, gold mining was on a small scale, and by 1885 Transvaal production was only .03 per cent of world production. A year later, however, the discovery of rich deposits on the Witwatersrand transformed the scene dramatically.

The Witwatersrand 'reef' was so big that within 12 years the South African Republic was the world's largest gold producer, with 27.5 per cent of the market. State revenue grew to £1.5 million in 1888-89, and the Cape Colony was replaced as the richest state in southern Africa. The chief drawback was that because the 'reef' lay hundreds of metres below the surface it proved difficult and expensive to work.

As with the diamond mines in Kimberley there was no place for the happy-go-lucky digger; only large, well-financed companies could afford to extract gold in paying quantities, and this made the rapid rise of the 'Randlords' inevitable. It also meant that labour costs had to be kept as low as possible. Thus the tragic paradox: gold brought untold wealth to the Transvaal but at the same time it created a large but under-privileged labour force.

To Kruger and his Government the gold rush was a welcome release from their financial problems, but the presence of large numbers of foreign mineworkers, businessmen and other professional people – or *Uitlanders* as they were known – threatened to overwhelm the 'indigenous' Afrikaners. The Uitlanders had no votes, and when Kruger handed out concessions to a variety of non-British individuals there was bound to be resentment. The imposition of mining and customs duties further exacerbated Uitlander resentment, providing British imperialists with a ready-made excuse for renewed intervention in Transvaal affairs.

In truth few of the Uitlanders were interested in the vote, but they resented the petty controls and the corruption of officialdom which made the task of making money harder. There was also an element of hypocrisy; the Republic officially deplored gold-mining as immoral, yet many of its citizens rushed to share in the profits. In 1895, for example, Kruger tried to divert trade to the new Delagoa Bay Railway by closing the Vaal drifts to Cape goods.

Cecil Rhodes saw the new-found wealth of the Transvaal as an obstacle to his dream of federation. His friendship with the powerful millionaire Alfred Beit, coupled with his own wealth, meant that he was uniquely placed to pursue such dreams. Shrewd investment in the Transvaal gold mining industry gave him great influence; by 1895 his New Consolidated Goldfields was the most important of the new monopolistic companies controlling the Witwatersrand – a situation which greatly added to his power.

Kruger was aware that failure to recognise Uitlander grievances would cause great mischief, but he was anxious to pre-

Above: 'High Change' on the Johannesburg Stock Exchange. One visitor described the Rand as Sodom and Gomorrah built on the foundations of Monte Carlo.

Right: The Eersteling Gold Mine was the first mine in the Transvaal. It operated from 1871 to 1880 and was declared a national monument in 1938.

Above left: Alfred Beit, one of the leading 'gold-bugs', was a powerful confederate of Cecil Rhodes in his grandiose plans.

Left: A *Cape Times* cartoon of November 1895 depicts Kruger as unpopular and isolated because of his favouritism towards non-*Uitlanders*.

serve the status quo at all costs. In 1890 he convened the Second Volksraad, with powers to legislate over Johannesburg and the Witwatersrand. Among the reforms that followed was the reduction of the residential qualification to two years, but this was nullified by two new rules: all legislation had to be ratified by the First Volksraad, and that body extended its own residential qualification from five to 14 years, and restricted the franchise to only those Uitlanders of 40 years of age or more.

The hope was that the Second Volksraad would provide the Uitlanders with an outlet for their political energies, while leaving the reins of government firmly in Afrikaner hands. It backfired because the majority of Uitlanders saw the changes as no more than window-dressing and refused to register as voters. Nothing, it seemed, could resolve the conundrum, but Rhodes as always thought that he had found the answer.

CECIL RHODES

While the biographical details of Cecil Rhodes are well known, he nevertheless remains something of an enigma. Born in Bishop's Stortford in England in 1853, the son of a vicar, Cecil John Rhodes first came to Natal when he was sent there for his health. When he arrived at the diamond fields in the early 1870s he was merely a junior to his brother Herbert and the other partners in the De Beers Company. Yet the sickly youngster was to prove more farsighted and imaginative than most of his elders and betters. It was a remarkable performance for a boy from a Hertfordshire vicarage.

With his fortune made at the Kimberley diamond diggings, Rhodes turned to politics, and was elected to the Cape Parliament as MP for Barkley West in 1881. His dream was for a federated self-governing South Africa under the British Crown. He differed from most British imperialists, however, in his conviction that the motor force for expansion must be the two colonies rather than the British Government. In Rhodes' eyes British Governments were inherently too slow-moving and above all, too fickle to execute a firm policy in southern Africa.

Annexation of the Transvaal and the Battle of Majuba put an end to any hope of co-operation between the two white races, but Rhodes persisted in efforts to win support from the moderate wing of Afrikaner politics. With the help of the Afrikaner Bond he became Prime Minister in 1890. His policy of expanding the Cape economy meant prosperity for the farming community, and J H Hofmeyr, the leader of the Bond, favoured any tendency to keep the two white races together.

Rhodes was obsessed with the balance of power between the

Right: Dick Lander's camp at Kimberley in 1872. Rhodes (seated with coffee pot) had been on the diamond fields for a year, sharing a claim with his brother.

Below: Rhodes, c1875, with a group of Highland officers.

Right: A watercolour of Rhodes at the height of his political career in Cape Town, painted by Mortimer Menpes.

Left: The jingoists saw Rhodes as the new Colossus, with dreams of a map painted red from Cape to Cairo. A *Punch* cartoon of the mid-1890s.

Right: Rhodes presides over a soup kitchen during the siege of Kimberley.

Below right: Rhodes addressing the shareholders of his British South Africa Company. 'Every man has his price'.

colonies and the Boer republics, and devoted his energies to blocking expansion of the South African Republic in particular. He used disturbances in Bechuanaland to persuade the British Government to annex the country and thereby eliminate any risk of an understanding between the Boers and the Germans to the west. Similarly his British South Africa Company was granted a charter in 1889 to administer Mashonaland and Matabeleland, thus blocking the Transvaal from expanding north of the Limpopo.

It was inevitable that a large section of the British public should admire Rhodes; his determination to 'paint the map red from Cape to Cairo' appealed to the prevailing spirit of jingoism. But dislike and criticism of his methods was not confined to the Afrikaners. Lieutenant-General Sir William Butler gave an unflattering description of him, recalling his sharp falsetto voice and his expression of 'peculiar mental pain'.

When his political career collapsed after the Jameson Raid Rhodes threw himself into Rhodesian affairs, showing great energy during the Ndebele rebellion. When the Anglo-Boer War broke out he was in Kimberley, and his presence gave the Boers additional reason to lay siege to the diamond fields.

The four-month siege of Kimberley highlighted the flaws in Rhodes's character. The garrison commander, Lieutenant-Colonel Kekewich, had the vast resources of De Beers at his disposal, and the Company's workshops turned out an artillery piece and even made shells. But Rhodes insisted on issuing orders independently, even communicating with the relieving forces. When his wilder schemes were rejected he threatened to surrender the town to the Boers, and any commander less patient than Kekewich would surely have been tempted to put Rhodes under arrest.

The tragic irony was that Rhodes had achieved something remarkable; he succeeded in kindling a unique spirit of colonial nationalism among the citizens of the Cape Colony. The Jameson Raid destroyed that dream just as it was beginning to come true. Had his ruthless ambition been confined to advancing the cause of Cape independence, he might have done the country much good, but in the end his belief that every man had a price led him to disaster. Today even his last achievement, Rhodesia, has been obliterated by the rising tide of African nationalism. His other legacy was a near-fatal rift between English- and Afrikaans-speakers. Yet paradoxically his financial empire continues to be a mainstay of South Africa's economy.

THE JAMESON RAID

Left: Rhodes at Groote Schuur, with his brother Frank, Alfred Beit and Dr Jameson.

The election of a Conservative Government in Britain in 1895 brought the Birmingham industrialist Joseph Chamberlain to the post of Colonial Secretary. He was able and energetic, and his firm response to Kruger's attempts to close the Transvaal's borders to Cape trade showed that he had no intention of withdrawing from Imperial responsibilities.

Rhodes, who was dying of tuberculosis, felt that his moment had come. By exploiting Uitlander grievances he planned to foment an uprising in the Transvaal. To 'assist' the insurrection he proposed that his deputy Dr Leander Starr Jameson (Administrator of the Chartered Company's territory), would invade the Transvaal and topple the republican Government. The Crown would then be forced to intervene, the Uitlanders would be enfranchised, and federation would follow smoothly.

Many of Chamberlain's enemies were later to claim that 'Pushful Joe' was the originator of the whole insane plan, but modern historians take a more lenient view. Clearly the Colonial Secretary learned at some point that an armed coup was being planned by Rhodes and his partner Alfred Beit. But instead of acting to stop this highly dangerous game Chamberlain did what other political opportunists have done before and since: he took care to 'know nothing'. That course allowed him to avoid implication if the plot failed, or to claim all the credit if it succeeded.

With the benefit of hindsight it is hard to believe that anyone thought that Dr Jameson's expedition could have succeeded. His force of 500 Rhodesian (BSA Company) Police waited on the Bechuanaland border at Pitsani in the last days of December 1895, but news of the Uitlander uprising never came. He was not to know that Chamberlain, suspecting that the Uitlanders would not act, had threatened to revoke the BSA Company's charter if Rhodes did not cancel the raid. On 29 December Jameson ordered his force across the border, hoping that

Above left: Joseph Chamberlain was a hero to the jingoistic British public. He gave tacit approval to Rhodes and Beit in their plans for the Raid.

Above: The schoolboy adventure came to an end as the Jameson Raiders were rounded up at Doornkop. No-one came to their aid.

Left: Caricature of 'Dr Jim' by 'Spy' in *Vanity Fair*, April 1896.

Right: The failure of the Raid was viewed unsympathetically by Britain's enemies, who professed outrage.

his action would stir the Uitlanders into rebellion.

In Johannesburg the plotters were divided and indecisive, some favouring an Uitlander-dominated republic rather than British annexation. There was also good reason to doubt whether the ordinary man-in-the-street was prepared to risk bloodshed to remedy his grievances.

Nor were the raiders very efficient. Their attempt to cut the telegraph line to Pretoria failed because they cut the wrong line, and as a result President Kruger and his military advisers were fully aware of Jameson's progress. Armed burghers started to harass the column as it approached Krugersdorp; and on 2 January the entire force was surrounded at Doornkop and forced to surrender. While Jameson and his men were led off ignominiously into captivity, the republic authorities swooped on the plotters in Johannesburg and arrested them.

Although Kruger dealt magnanimously with the raiders and their accomplices, sending Jameson and five officers to Britain for trial and fining the Reform Committee members, the raid did incalculable harm. Rhodes resigned as premier

and the Afrikaner Bond severed all ties with him, leaving the Bond clear to win the next election. More far-reaching, the Free State now committed itself totally to the Transvaal cause, convinced that the British intended to destroy both republics.

Chamberlain escaped more lightly than he should have, not least because he was a member of the Parliamentary Committee of Inquiry convened to investigate the circumstances of the raid. He was able to persuade Beit and Rhodes to suppress certain cables, in return for a promise not to revoke the BSA Company's charter, and Jameson also promised to keep quiet. Even more crucial, the Imperial Secretary at the Cape, Sir Graham Bower, loyally acted out the role of scapegoat, pretending that he had not told Chamberlain about the impending raid.

Far left: The Jameson Raiders cut the wrong telegraph wire. As a result the Pretoria authorities knew exactly where they were.

Right: Rhodes as a character from a *Struwwelpeter* alphabet – 'The Diamond Mine-R'.

The Diamond Mine R.

R is Rhodes with beating heart,
  Jim's upset his apple cart;
Rhodes is in a dreadful fright
For he will not get a Beit;
O it was a nasty slip—
All poor Rhodes will get 's—the pip.

(18)

Above left: Pretoria in the mid-1890s, with tents and wagons of visiting Boer families.

Left: Dr Jameson (centre) and some of his unsuccessful Raiders on their return to England in 1898.

This farrago of lies and half-truths might not have saved the Colonial Secretary had not the Kaiser chosen to make one of his unfortunate appearances on the international stage. A telegram to President Kruger congratulating him on his escape from the British plot roused the British public to fury. Suddenly Chamberlain and Jameson were heroes, and the Liberal opposition felt unable to press their advantage. Not for nothing was the Committee of Inquiry known to many people as the 'Lying-in-State'.

The raid put the Boer republics on a collision course with Great Britain. The humiliation of Majuba and the Liberals was now joined by the humiliation of Chamberlain and the Conservatives. The last chance for the British to salvage anything from the long series of mistakes, blunders and lost opportunities was gone. Within a few years the Boers and British would again be at war.

THE SECOND ANGLO-BOER WAR
OPENING SHOTS

After the Jameson Raid relations between Britain and the Boer republics deteriorated rapidly. Chamberlain was determined to influence the course of events in the Transvaal and Kruger was equally determined to stop him. Although he publicly avowed that a war against the Transvaal would be prolonged, acrimonious and expensive, Chamberlain's relentless pressure made such an outcome more and more likely. He wanted federation, not war, but he managed to implant the idea in the mind of Sir Alfred Milner, the new High Commissioner, that Kruger should be shown to be the aggressor.

Milner was chosen by Chamberlain for his outstanding success as an imperial administrator. His work in Egypt marked him as the shining example of the new type of imperialist, strong-minded but methodical and professional. His intellectual abilities were phenomenal but he suffered from one fault above all: he was unable to accept other people's views.

Milner's grand design required considerable military strength to overawe the two republics, but British public opinion would not have permitted a huge build-up of troops. Nor were the Boers easily overawed, with Majuba and other successes behind them. The Jameson Raid had alerted the Transvaal Government to the weakness of its defences. At a cost of £1 million Paul Kruger re-equipped the Army, importing 37,000 Mauser magazine rifles, sufficient to give each burgher a second rifle. By 1899 the Republic could muster 25,000 men, to which would be added 15,000 burghers from the Free State. Against this formidable force of mounted

Above: Sir Alfred Milner was appointed High Commissioner following his successful administration of Egypt. He was determined to secure British supremacy over the Boers.

Right: One of the Creusot 15cm 'Long Tom' artillery pieces bought for the *Staatsartillerie*. This schoolbook was published by a French pro-Boer society for free distribution to children.

Above: Boer 'roving field artillery' attacking Mafeking.

Left: Boer scouts posing with their new 7.7mm Mauser magazine-loading rifles.

Below: Sir George White VC. Many of Buller's problems were caused by White's impetuous stupidity.

infantry and a modern artillery corps the British had only 10,000 troops divided between the Cape and Natal. Warnings from the Commander-in-Chief, Lieutenant-General Sir William Butler about the inadequacy of his garrisons for any form of offensive operations were dismissed as 'pro-Boer' and 'pessimistic', and his resignation was accepted. In fact Butler tried to prevent the war by deliberately not asking for any reinforcements.

Milner's efforts to precipitate hostilities were nearly frustrated by last-minute concessions by Paul Kruger and the Volksraad, but suddenly the old President played into his hands. On 9 September Kruger learned that large numbers of British reinforcements were on their way, and on 9 October an ultimatum was presented to the British Government, giving them 48 hours to withdraw all additional forces. Such was the over-confidence in London that most people expressed fears

Above: 'Long Cecil' was built by the De Beers workshops during the Siege of Kimberley. It fired 28lb shells.

Right: Boers from one of the commandos besieging Ladysmith. These operations frittered away their strength without producing a decisive victory.

that the Boers would not fight.

Although the Boers were determined to take the offensive they repeated the errors of 1881 by besieging unimportant garrisons in Kimberley, Mafeking and Ladysmith. But the British Major-General Sir William Penn-Symons had moved his 4500 troops up to Dundee, where they were exposed to attack by the Boers. When this occurred the British were taken completely by surprise, Penn-Symons was killed, and his troops were only extricated with difficulty.

The British were now badly off-balance. The local commander Sir George White bungled his attempt to halt the Boer advance after suffering 1200 casualties, and allowed his Natal Field Force to be trapped in Ladysmith. By 2 November the town was cut off. It could have been the moment for a decisive blow by General Joubert against the British, but instead of destroying the remaining forces in Natal, Joubert's burghers settled down to a leisurely siege.

Mafeking and Kimberley were also besieged, tying down Boer strength for no discernible military advantage. Both places had symbolic value, however; Mafeking had been a supply depot for the Jameson Raid, while Kimberley was the home of Cecil Rhodes and the diamond mines.

The hope that Britain would be forced to negotiate by a snap victory proved a delusion. British public opinion had been whipped up in a way that had never been possible before, and there was no support for any quick retreat. Nor was there a decisive defeat to match Majuba, only a sense of outrage at what was seen as poor generalship. There was also the romantic appeal of a siege, with naval guns rushed up from Durban. The British Government was playing for high stakes and the public mood was more bellicose than it had been for many years, making a negotiated peace almost unthinkable.

THE SECOND ANGLO-BOER WAR
BLACK WEEK

The British had good strategic reasons for relieving Kimberley; such a move would remove a Boer threat to the railway network in the Cape Midlands, a prerequisite for offensive operations by the reinforcements now pouring into the Cape. The new Commander in Chief, General Sir Redvers Buller VC, intended to deploy an entire army corps in the Cape. While Sir George White's forces defended Natal the army corps would use the railways to advance through the Free State to Bloemfontein and then on to Pretoria. But by the time Buller landed in Cape Town at the end of October 1899 the two colonies were virtually defenceless and White was trapped in Ladysmith. The Corps was immediately broken up to provide reinforce-

ments for Natal, leaving the forces in the Cape only loosely co-ordinated. Lieutenant-General Lord Methuen's attempt to relieve Kimberley ran into trouble at Belmont, where his troops won an expensive victory. Two days later the Naval Brigade suffered heavy casualties at Graspan, and it was clear that every piece of high ground would be similarly contested.

Methuen won an even more expensive victory when crossing the Modder River on 28 November. Although he was within 20 miles of Kimberley supply problems and a shortage of cavalry and mounted infantry made it impossible to relieve the town. By the time the force was ready to march again General de la Rey had reinforced his position on the Spyt-

Above: General Sir Redvers Buller, VC, was appointed Commander-in-Chief to succeed Sir William Butler in 1899.

Left: To match the Boer 'Long Tom' 15cm guns the Royal Navy improvised carriages for guns such as this naval 4.7-inch (12cm) gun as well as 12-pounder (7.6cm) and 6-inch (15.2cm) guns stripped from cruisers at Simon's Town.

Left: The death of Lieutenant Frederick Roberts at Colenso while trying to save the guns, 15 December 1899.

Above: At Magersfontein the Guards and Highlanders tried a reckless frontal assault on a well-prepared Boer position.

Above: The British were supported by lumbering wagon trains, a great hindrance when trying to match the mounted Boer riflemen.

Right: Lord Roberts was one of Britain's most successful generals. His appointment marked British determination to settle the war.

Left: A French cartoon showing a Boer spanking Queen Victoria expressed widespread sympathy for the Boers.

fontein and Magersfontein ridges.

The Battle of Magersfontein on 11 December was a disaster for the British, who suffered over 1000 casualties, as against less than 200 Boers killed and wounded. Reckless frontal assaults against a poorly reconnoitred position had given the Boer marksmen a comparatively easy victory, but Magersfontein had wider significance – Britain's finest troops, the Guards and Highland Brigades, had once more been given a thrashing by a 'rabble' of farmers.

To make matters worse General Gatacre had failed in his attempt to evict the Free Staters from Stormberg the day before. This railway junction on the Bloemfontein-East London line was strategically important and Gatacre tried a night march from Molteno, timed to end in a dawn assault. Careless planning added to the length of the march, and at first light the column was ambushed while still tightly bunched. The exhausted troops were no match for the Boers,

and in the confused withdrawal some 600 were captured.

In Natal Buller's massive offensive to relieve Ladysmith got underway. To reach the town he had to make a ten-mile approach across open country to the fast-flowing Thukela River, a formidable obstacle. General Louis Botha was defending the north bank, with 12 commandos, a dozen guns of the State Artillery and a strong force of Johannesburg Police, all concentrated on a front only six-and-a-half miles wide.

Once again the British attacked without reconnoitring the position fully, and made another series of suicidal frontal assaults. By 0700 hours on the morning of 15 December the entire attacking force of infantry and artillery had been pinned down, and four hours later a disheartened Buller ordered the operation abandoned. Next day he ordered the entire force to fall back on Chievely and Frere, having suffered 1100 casualties; the Boer losses totalled only 40.

The Battle of Colenso coming so soon after Magersfontein and Stormberg caused the British newspapers to talk of 'Black Week'. The sequence of disasters not only blighted Buller's reputation but also signalled a change in British perceptions of the war. No more talk was heard of 'punitive expeditions' or minor colonial campaigns. For South Africa the new mood was to have tragic consequences; the British were seized with a renewed sense of purpose and patriotic fervour. Determination to redeem national honour was now the prime objective, not just in the British Isles but throughout the Empire.

Although Buller remained in command in Natal a new Commander in Chief was appointed, Field-Marshal Lord Roberts, with Lord Kitchener as Chief of Staff. Neither leader had any experience of South African conditions but they were both experienced soldiers, and their appointments reflected the seriousness with which the British Government regarded the situation. Crushing the two Republics was now the only military objective, and pro-Boer sympathy was muted.

H.P.WILSON

Above: Lord Kitchener, fresh from his victory at Omdurman, was appointed Chief of Staff to Roberts.

Left: The loss of Roberts' only son while trying to save his guns at Colenso was a sad blow. They became a rare example of a father and son both winning the Victoria Cross.

THE SECOND ANGLO-BOER WAR
DESTRUCTION OF THE REPUBLICS

It was to take Buller another two months to hammer his way through the Boer defences around Ladysmith, but the siege was eventually raised on 28 February 1900. Coming in the wake of both General French's success in getting through to Kimberley on 15 February and Kitchener's expensive victory over Cronje at Paardeberg two days later, it seemed to the British that victory was within their grasp.

Paardeberg was the first major defeat for the Boers. The loss of 4000 burghers was a harsh blow, and strategically the collapse of the 'Western Front' removed a major threat to the Cape Colony. For the British, Cronje's surrender on the anniversary of Majuba went a long way to compensate for Kitchener's needlessly costly assaults.

Roberts' entry into Bloemfontein on 10 March would, he hoped, knock the Orange Free State out of the war. But the capture of both republics' capital cities had no effect, for the Boers placed little store in the possession of towns. The offer of a general amnesty had little effect, although some burghers handed in obsolete weapons. The strength of Boer resistance lay in the mobility and firepower of the commandos, not in conventional army formations.

On 17 March the two presidents held a *Krygsraad* or council of war at Kroonstad. Kruger was ill and many Boers were beginning to lose heart, but the old man made a passionate speech, reminding the burghers of their mission as God's chosen people. Steyn talked of international sympathy for the Boer cause, but the new Commandant-General of the Free State forces, Christiaan de Wet, brought proceedings down to a practical level. He proposed a leave-period of ten days to per-

Above: General Piet Cronje after his surrender, accompanied by Roberts' ADC, Captain Watermeyer of the Cape Town Highlanders.

Left: The relief of Ladysmith was not marked by the frantic revelry of Mafeking Night, but it raised British morale and was an important turning point.

Top: Royal Artillery crossing the Modder River at Paardeberg Drift, during the pursuit of Cronje.

Above: General Christiaan de Wet took command in the dark days after Paardeberg and the fall of Bloemfontein.

Left: Roberts entering Bloemfontein in March 1900.

Daily Express

NO. 23.   LONDON, SATURDAY, MAY 19, 1900.   ONE HALFPENNY.

WHEN SHALL THEIR GLORY FADE?

HISTORY'S MOST HEROIC DEFENCE ENDS IN TRIUMPH.

THE BOERS' LAST GRIP LOOSENED.

MAFEKING AND BADEN-POWELL'S GALLANT BAND SET FREE.

"LET ME TELL MOTHER."

HOW THE "EXPRESS" FIRST GAVE THE NEWS

TO BADEN-POWELL'S HOME.

PRETORIA, Friday.

It is officially announced that when the laagers and forts around Mafeking had been severely bombarded the siege was abandoned by the Boers.

WESTWARD HO!

EVERYBODY KNEW.

THE RIGHT WORDS.

Above: The Battle of Paardeberg. Balloons were used for reconnaissance, but required scarce draught animals, and were not a great success.

Left: The hysterical reaction of the *Daily Express* to the relief of Mafeking was typical. However Baden-Powell did tie up Boer commandos who would have been useful elsewhere.

Right: 'B-P' as seen by the *Natal Mercury* after the relief.

mit all burghers to go home; the best men would return refreshed and rested, and those who did not return would be no loss to the fighting strength of the commandos.

It was de Wet, and to a lesser extent de la Rey, who transformed the character of the war. Their ruthlessness and dedication cut across many cherished traditions. The ponderous wagon-loads of women and children that had been one of the causes of Cronje's defeat at Paardeberg, would go, leaving the menfolk free to harass the British supply-lines.

Meanwhile Roberts was pushing his columns into the Transvaal to bring an end to resistance. Despite a severe outbreak of enteric (typhoid) fever, by the beginning of May 1900 he had 70,000 soldiers and 178 guns north of the Orange River. The great push began on 3 May, in conjunction with

Below: Lord Roberts and his staff planning the advance.

Bottom: Although Roberts sanctioned a tough policy of farm-burning, he avoided the odium which clung to Kitchener because of the concentration camps.

a methodical push by Buller in Natal. In all some 100,000 Imperial troops were facing barely 30,000 Boers.

Against such odds the Free Staters and Transvaalers could do little, but they conceded ground as slowly as they could, blowing up bridges and railways as they went. On 12 May Roberts entered Kroonstadt, but the exhausted infantry, mounted infantry and cavalry needed ten days' rest to recuperate and to allow the supply-trains to catch up.

On 16 May the news of the relief of Mafeking triggered off an outburst of hysterical joy out of all proportion to the importance of the town. London had a night of crazy 'mafficking', and Colonel Baden-Powell and his band of military amateurs became heroes overnight. The most that can be claimed for 'B-P's' efforts was his success in tying down as many as 10,000 Boers during the crucial days at the start of the war. For the rest of the time the town was subjected to the same lethargic siege warfare demonstrated by the Boers at Kimberley and Ladysmith.

Roberts crossed the Vaal on 24 May, and six days later Johannesburg surrendered. The spirit of the Transvaalers was at a very low ebb, and had Roberts only known, he might have achieved a surrender. President Kruger left Pretoria on 30 May. The 26,000 weary sunburnt soldiers who entered the

Right: Roberts' main column of 42,000 men and 117 guns invaded the Orange Free State in May 1900.

Below: On 'Mournful Monday' Sir George White's troops were driven back into Ladysmith. The Natal Field Force was virtually neutralized, unavailable to defend Natal.

Transvaal capital on 5 June could be forgiven for thinking that it was all over. Some 38,000 had marched out of Bloemfontein, but disease, battle casualties, lack of horses and, above all, the need to guard 300 miles of lines of communica-tions accounted for the missing 12,000 troops. Yet for the embattled republics the loss of their material possessions was only the beginning of a new struggle, more destructive and costly to both sides than anything yet seen.

THE SECOND ANGLO-BOER WAR
ATTRITION

The war seemed over on 1 June 1900, when the Transvaal military and political leaders were ready to surrender. It took a stinging rebuke from President Steyn, who was determined that the Free State would not give in, to stiffen their resolve. In Steyn's view the Transvaalers had involved his republic and the Cape Boers in ruin, and should therefore not be ready to surrender as soon as the war reached their borders.

Simultaneously Christiaan de Wet and his brother Piet took the offensive, capturing over 500 Imperial Yeomanry at Lindley. Within a week the two de Wets were to capture over 1000 men, a fraction of the British forces in South Africa but a dramatic example of how effective guerrilla tactics could be. Chastened by Steyn's telegram and cheered by good news at last, Botha regrouped and a week later had amassed 6000 men and 23 guns. Even though they failed to hold Diamond Hill (also known as Donkerhoek) east of Pretoria they held up the advance and melted away just as the net closed about them.

This was the last of the set-piece battles. From now on de Wet's strategy was to prevail: the commandos would remain separated to maintain mobility and they would avoid costly actions against superior forces. There were to be disasters such as the capture of 3000 burghers under Commandant Prinsloo on 29 July, but Botha, Smuts, de la Rey and de Wet kept at large, eluding the slow-moving columns. In August Kitchener had 11,000 men in five columns trying to pin de Wet against a defence line manned by another 18,000, yet the quarry always found an unguarded gap, or simply moved faster than its opponents.

Above: The South African Light Horse marching through the streets of Cape Town on their way to the front.

Left: Boers posing for the camera behind a temporary *schanze* or rifle pit. Smokeless powder and a rapid rate of fire made the Mauser breechloading rifle even more deadly in the hands of Boer marksmen.

Above: The Imperial Yeomanry were only one of a number of volunteer mounted infantry formations raised to remedy the shortcomings of the Regular Army.

Right: Campaigning in South Africa had its discomforts, including extremes of heat and cold.

In the Transvaal it was easier to harry President Kruger and his Government for they were tied to the Delagoa Bay railway link. But once Kruger crossed the Portuguese border on his way to exile, Botha and his commandants were free to return to the offensive, moving northwards before the British could cut them off.

In October 1900 the British reorganised their forces, sending Buller home and absorbing the Natal Field Force into a unified army command. Lord Roberts was also anxious to go home, believing that his successor, Kitchener, would have little to do beyond mopping-up. With garrisons in all the major towns and cities, the railways under their control and the veld covered by 'flying columns' of infantry and cavalry, the British were sure that the war had degenerated into nothing more than a police action.

Late that month President Steyn and General Botha met to map out policy. Commandos would operate mainly from their home areas, although it was recognised that Kitchener was likely to respond by burning any farms thought to be harbouring guerrillas. The two leaders proposed to reduce this risk by raiding the Cape and Natal. There, it was argued, the authorities would not dare to burn farms, since the presence of Boer commandos might incite colonial Afrikaners to join the cause.

Kitchener had inherited an entirely new kind of war for which neither he nor his army was trained. While the one-time 'hawk' Sir Alfred Milner now urged gradual pacification to avoid further bitterness, Kitchener wanted to bring the war to a close by direct military action. He ordered that all non-

Right: President Kruger in Paris, beginning his self-imposed exile. He would never see his beloved Transvaal again.

Below: The French cartoonist Henri Somm's sardonic view of the British hunt for de Wet.

combatants, including women, children and servants be removed from outlying farms; burghers surrendering voluntarily would be allowed to live with their families. These camps, set up near railway junctions where both supply and protection would be eased, became known as 'concentration' camps when English Radical critics of the policy drew parallels with the notorious Spanish *reconcentrado* camps in Cuba.

Despite the new harshness the war did not end. Instead it continued into 1901. Not even a successful raid into the Cape by Hertzog provoked an uprising, and Botha's plan to raid Natal had been thwarted. Kitchener attempted to negotiate a settlement, meeting with Botha at Middelburg on 28 February but the terms were not acceptable. Neither side was free to manoeuvre; Kitchener could not agree with Milner on amnesty terms, and Botha could not be certain that the Free State burghers would surrender.

The British were now reduced to a policy of attrition, using sheer numbers to wear down the manpower of the commandos. A 'scorched earth' policy would deprive them of their means of subsistence. Eventually 24,000 burghers would be sent as prisoners-of-war to Ceylon and St Helena, while many of their dependents would be interned. Yet such was their determination and hardiness that the burghers fought on for another year.

THE SECOND ANGLO-BOER WAR
TO THE BITTER END

The policy of putting 'refugees' into camps was sanctioned by Lord Roberts in September 1900, but it was Kitchener who ordered wholesale clearance of Boer non-combatants in specified areas of intensive guerrilla activity. There were eventually more than 40 concentration camps, housing 116,000 Boer dependents, in addition to another 60 camps containing a similar number of black servants.

Much has been written about the concentration camps and the effect they had on their unfortunate inmates, but the worst charge that can be laid at the door of the British military authorities is one of neglect and insensitivity. Given that parts of the country were reverting to desert, the women and children left behind on the farms would have faced starvation, so that moving them to camps was intended as a humane gesture. But Kitchener's tidy, economical mind dreamed up two ration-scales, including a lower one for families whose menfolk had not yet surrendered. Even after this unpleasant distinction had been removed and such 'luxuries' as meat and vegetables had been restored, the rations were still much poorer than those authorised for the Army. There was also the plight of black servants, all but forgotten in their own camps, where the mortality rates remained high.

Officers with no experience of dealing with large numbers of internees suddenly found themselves swamped by medical problems, not only births and infantile diseases but also the by-products of malnutrition and poor hygiene. It is to Kitchener's discredit that he dismissed any criticism of the camps by saying that they were not intended to be comfortable. They provided a minimum, and in any case everything was under

Above: Emily Hobhouse is remembered today for her unpopular campaign to draw the attention of the British public to the plight of Boer non-combatants.

Left: One of the British Army-run camps for Boer women and children and their black servants, left homeless by the policy of burning farms.

control and the inmates were happy. It is perhaps too much to ask if Kitchener had ever visited one of these camps.

Without the work of Emily Hobhouse it is probable that nothing would have changed. This middle-aged Cornish spinster had previously been secretary to the South African Reconciliation Committee and in June 1900 she organised a protest against British policy in South Africa. With the backing of Radical politicians she persuaded Milner to allow her to visit

the concentration camps in January 1901, and what she saw appalled her. The harrowing details and statistics provided by Emily Hobhouse were used by critics of the Salisbury Government's conduct of the war. Despite attempts by Kitchener and the War Office to conceal the scale of mortality and the truth about conditions, the British Government was eventually forced to capitulate, and the Fawcett Commission's proposals were put into effect to remedy the worst abuses.

The plight of the menfolk, however, deteriorated. Kitchener's huge network of blockhouses gradually squeezed the commandos out of important areas, enabling the Army to chase them like game in huge 'drives' across the veld. Towards the end it required a small-scale pitched battle to cross a railway line. By 1902 there were 18,000 blockhouses manned by 50,000 troops, guarding bridges and vital rail-links.

Although Smuts led another successful large-scale raid into the Cape, a similar effort by Botha to invade Natal was defeated. The commandos were still dangerous. General de la Rey captured Lord Methuen at Tweebosch in March 1902 but the exchange-rate was poor; between December 1901 and February 1902 the 'drives' accounted for 4000 Boers. Starvation and shortage of ammunition were now acute; some burghers were half-naked and relied on captured clothing and weapons to keep going. It was sheer exhaustion that brought the Boers to the conference table in April 1902.

As at Middelburg Kitchener and Milner could not agree; Milner opposed the scorched-earth policy but wanted the Boers to surrender unconditionally, whereas Kitchener wanted to

Above: The Boers attacked British supply-lines, particularly vulnerable railway lines.

Left: Blockhouses were built to protect railway lines and bridges from attack. Kitchener built a huge network to wear down the Boers, but it tied up large numbers of troops.

The Bloemfontein Post.

JUNE 1st, 1902.

SPECIAL.

PEACE

Officially Declared.

DETAILS LATER.

Left: The 'Peace Special' edition of the *Bloemfontein Post* celebrates the end of a singularly bitter war.

Below: The capture of Lord Methuen at Tweebosch in 1902 showed that the Boers remained dangerous to the end.

bring the hugely expensive campaign to an end quickly. But once peace broke out it was hard to stop. The first talks began on 11 April, with Schalk Burger, Botha, Steyn, Botha, de Wet and other delegates coming to the British headquarters in Pretoria. Out of these 'talks about talks' the Boer leaders agreed to elect 60 national delegates for a full peace conference at Vereeniging in mid-May.

Although some of the *bittereinders* talked of fighting on there was little support, and further conflict would only deepen the rift opening up in the *volk*. A combination of legal skill and diplomacy ensured a workable formula. If the Boers accepted the authority of the Crown, self-government would follow 'when circumstances permitted'. All acts of war committed in good faith would be covered by an amnesty, Cape rebels (except leaders) would be disenfranchised but not imprisoned, the Dutch language would be allowed in courts and schools, no war tax would be levied on Boer property, and money would be available to rebuild and restock farms.

The cost was appalling: the Free State and the Transvaal lost an estimated 4000 burghers killed in action, and 26,000 non-combatants from disease in the concentration camps. The British lost 21,000 troops and the total cost was estimated at £220 million. It had been a very expensive victory.

REBUILDING THE NATION

Left: Sepia print of a Boer family returning to its farm as resettlement gathers momentum. £3 million was voted by the British to rebuild and restock farms.

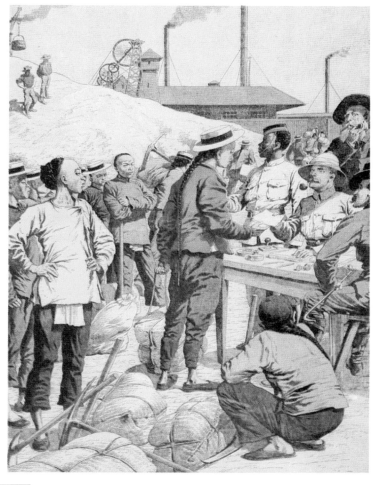

Below: Indentured Chinese labourers were imported to get the gold mines working again. Without the revenue from the mines reconstruction would have taken much longer.

The peace agreement which concluded the Second Anglo-Boer War was, as Milner said, an unusual agreement, one that extracted no indemnity from the defeated, an acceptance of British sovereignty although with a promise of self-rule, and a promise of £3 million to compensate the losers. But something different was needed if anything positive was to emerge from the blunders of the past. Although Milner's attempt to woo Botha, de la Rey and Smuts to serve on the Transvaal Legislative Council failed, his 'kindergarten' of young Oxford graduates created the framework for efficient administration. Their first priority was to get the gold mines working again to provide prosperity. New schools were established in the style of British public schools as a means of strengthening pro-British elements.

A huge resettlement scheme was necessary to get both blacks and whites back where they had been before the war, but a plan by Milner to create a new English immigrant farming community failed dismally. Government schools were to teach the English language only, while Afrikaans was firmly discouraged. Such blatant discrimination did much to revive Afrikaner cultural aspirations.

One thing united the whites, the belief that it had been a 'white man's war', and that South Africa should remain a 'white man's country'. For those non-white leaders who had looked to the British for some improvement in their status this attitude found little sympathy. Black leaders like J T Jabavu hoped to achieve their aims by a gradual approach and tried to join the white political process. In Natal the Reverend John L Dube helped to focus black aspirations, as did Gandhi for Indians. Black newspapers such as *Imvo Zabantsundu* (African Opinion) and *Ilanga Lase Natal* (the Natal Sun) con-

Top: Photograph of the Reverend John L Dube who became an influential black leader in Natal. He founded Ohlange High School and edited *Ilanga Lase Natal*.

Above: Photograph of J T Jabavu. He edited *Imvo Zabantsundu*, but the British closed it under martial law regulations during the Anglo-Boer War.

Right: Photograph of Generals de Wet, de la Rey and Botha on their way to England after the war.

tinued to give expression to black disgust at the British failure to improve their lot.

The gold mines were soon back in full production but the need to go deeper and the high cost of refining gold from lower-grade ore was pushing up production costs. Faced with difficulties in recruiting black labour for low wages the Chamber of Mines endorsed a plan to recruit Chinese indentured labour to make good the shortfall.

The first of some 63,000 Chinese arrived on three-year contracts in June 1904. Although they proved hard workers and helped immeasurably to restore the health of the mining industry at a critical time, there was great political opposition to 'coolie labour', both in South Africa and outside. In 1907 the last indentured Chinese were repatriated, by which time the mining industry was well on the road to recovery.

Afrikaner political activity was dormant for only a short while. The death of Paul Kruger at Clarens in Switzerland in July 1904 and the return of his body to Pretoria caused a new consciousness among Afrikaners, but in fact the wartime leaders were still influential. Grievances over repatriation, discrimination in schools and the allocations of relief all kept

the sense of separate identity alive. The movement *Het Volk* was formally constituted as early as January 1905, and was followed six months later by *Orangia Unie* in what was now the Orange River Colony.

Although the British Government honoured its promise to rebuild and restock the farms, agricultural recovery was slow. Many rural Afrikaners began drifting steadily into the towns in the hope of finding work, and a new class of 'poor whites' emerged. Afrikaner political organisations exploited the sense of grievance skilfully. Milner's policy of English-medium education was countered by demands for Christian National Education, and a new Second Language Movement which promoted Afrikaans as a vehicle for cultural renewal.

To rebuild the industrial sinews of the country it was decided to expand and modernise the railways. Although Milner's Customs Union was not a success he combined the Free State and Transvaal rail networks into a single Central South African Railway. Although the Union achieved its aim of reducing the Transvaal's dependence on the Delagoa Bay link it unleashed fresh rivalry between the Cape and Natal. Settlement of the quarrel was to prove hard to achieve.

Above: Ex-President Kruger's coffin arriving at Cape Town docks in 1904, following his death in Switzerland.

Left: Paul Kruger's body lying in state in the *chapelle ardente* aboard the SS *Batavier*, anchored in Cape Town.

PART III

THE STRUGGLE FOR NATIONHOOD

CREATING THE UNION OF SOUTH AFRICA

The election of a Liberal Government in Britain in 1906 speeded the process of unification. Self-government for the Transvaal and Free State had already been conceded, bringing Louis Botha of *Het Volk* and Abraham Fischer of *Orangia Unie* to power as respective premiers.

The British Government's aim was to consolidate all four colonies into a single dominion along the lines of Canada and Australia. There were a number of sound and pressing reasons for this, quite apart from the need to strengthen Empire ties. Strategically the Cape sea route was not vital to British naval power, but secure possession of the base at Simonstown would become important if war should break out between the European Powers. Milner's Customs Union of 1903 was a mishmash of differing tariffs and freight costs, and it was important for a united country to raise its own defence forces in order to cope with any internal problems. The Bambatha Rebellion of 1906 had been put down by the Natal militia and volunteers with heavy black casualties, but Imperial troops had been called in to help control the gold miners' strike in 1907.

Milner's successor, Lord Selborne, speeded up the process by putting his name to the so-called Selborne Memorandum.

This document, outlining all the arguments for unification, met with widespread support. A National Convention was convened in Durban in 1908 under the presidency of Sir Henry de Villiers, Chief Justice of the Cape Colony, and in less than a year a draft constitution had been produced, although some issues were conveniently overlooked or set aside.

The franchise question was settled in the short term by permitting each member-state to retain the system pertaining before union: blacks and Coloureds had a qualified franchise in the Cape but no vote in the Free State, Natal or Transvaal. Membership of the House of Assembly and the Senate was open only to whites. To avoid rivalry there would be three capitals: Cape Town (legislative), Pretoria (administrative) and Bloemfontein (judicial).

Although the majority of white South Africans were enthusiastic about the proposed South Africa Bill many blacks, Coloureds and Indians were dismayed to see the colour bar enshrined in the draft legislation. The upshot was that a rival 'South African Native Convention' was held at Bloemfontein in 1909; support for federation was voiced and it was resolved that the Cape franchise should be adopted throughout the country.

Left: Delegates to the Inter-Colonial Conference at Pretoria in June 1908, one of the milestones leading to Union.

Above: General Louis Botha and his wife at their house in Pretoria. Arguably the most talented of the Boer guerrilla leaders, he devoted the rest of his life to reunification.

Pages 114-115: South African troops at a railhead during the South West Africa Campaign in 1915.

Right: Jan Hofmeyr (1894-1948) put his brilliant intellectual and administrative abilities at the disposal of Smuts. He did much to secure the coalition between Hertzog and Smuts, and virtually ran the country in World War II.

In mid-1909 J H Hofmeyr and his delegation took the draft Bill to London. A second delegation led by the ex-premier of the Cape W P Schreiner and including African and Coloured leaders also went to London to plead the case for more protection for black interests, and Gandhi and the Indians made similar representations, but neither delegation met with success. On 20 September the unamended South Africa Act received the royal assent.

It was clear that Louis Botha commanded the most support among whites, although John X Merriman would probably have commanded more black and Coloured support had it been canvassed, so Botha was asked by the new Governor-General to form the first Union Government.

Despite the enthusiasm for Union the rifts between capital and labour, and between white and black had not healed. Under the leadership of J B M Hertzog the notion of 'South Africa for the Afrikaner' was promoted; Botha and Smuts, on the other hand, believed that partnership with the English-speakers and prosperity within the Empire would in the long run benefit the Afrikaners more.

In 1912 the African National Congress was formed to voice black opinions, although Jabavu persevered with his own South African Races Congress. White labour was also under pressure from the employers, and unrest brought about two strikes in 1913-14. Smuts reacted quickly in 1914, deporting nine railway union leaders to Europe.

In 1913 legislation was passed that was to dramatically widen the rift between whites and blacks in South Africa. In 1912 Hertzog had been excluded from the Cabinet, but a revised version of his draft act to restrict the amount of land available to blacks was steered through Parliament by J W Sauer. The Natives Land Act of 1913 had the effect of excluding blacks from 'white' areas or forcing them into the labour market on white terms.

Far left: The Hon W P Schreiner led the South African Party before the Anglo-Boer War, becoming Prime Minister of the Cape Colony.

Left: General James Barrie Munnik Hertzog was a doughty fighter for the rights of the Afrikaner Nation, but he hoped to protect English-speakers' rights as well.

Below: The proclamation of martial law at the Drill Hall in Cape Town during the rail strike in February 1914.

Above: Crowds of striking miners in Bree Street, Johannesburg during the 1913 strike. In all 21 strikers were killed in clashes with the police.

Left: Carrying food to outlying UDF units during the 1914 rail strike. Nine foreign-born strike leaders were deported to Europe.

THE 1914 REBELLION

The passage of the South African Defence Act in 1912 established the Union Defence Force. Apart from internal security the only perceived external threat was from the Germans in South West Africa. When the First World War broke out in August 1914 it brought South Africa as a member of the British Empire automatically into conflict with Germany, and almost as a formality the Government offered to assume the responsibilities that would normally fall to the Imperial garrison.

The certainty that South African troops would be used against South West Africa brought to a head grievances which had been simmering among many Afrikaners, particularly among senior military officers. Apart from hankerings after long-lost independence there was resentment about unequal opportunities, and probably an echo of the old Irish dictum, 'England's adversity is Ireland's opportunity'. What is certain is that some senior officers, including Generals Maritz and Kemp and a number of Boer War veterans discussed as early as 1912 the possibility of using their positions in the Union Defence Force to restore the old republics should an opportunity arise.

In mid-August 1914 the plotters decided on a *coup d'état*, using the elderly and respected General 'Koos' de la Rey as a figurehead. Although details were vague Maritz was instructed to arrange a meeting between the German authorities and Commandant-General Beyers. Subsequently both Beyers and Kemp resigned their commissions to free themselves of

any obligation to their oaths of loyalty, but fate took a hand. While Beyers was driving de la Rey to a military camp at Potchefstroom (it has always been claimed that the old general was to be used to subvert Government troops from their allegiance) he was challenged by a police roadblock. Assuming that the police were aware of the plot, Beyers refused to stop, and in the firing a stray bullet killed General de la Rey. The police were in fact hunting for a gang of dangerous criminals but the tragic misunderstanding caused the plotters to lose the initiative at a crucial moment.

On 9 October Maritz took command, leading over 1000 Citizen Force men across the frontier to join the Germans. Two days later the South African Government proclaimed martial law and called up its burghers for the last time. Beyers went into open rebellion and was joined by de Wet. At first the rebels seemed to win support, but the days of guerrilla warfare on horseback were over. De Wet's son was killed and finally the old man himself was beaten. For a while de Wet's skill enabled him to escape capture, but Government troops hunted him and his horsemen down in motor cars, a symbolic reminder that the old days had gone forever.

A week later Beyers was trapped, and while attempting to swim his horse across the Vaal River he fell off and was drowned. Maritz failed to spark off rebellion in the Cape but he and Kemp joined forces and scored a victory at Nous in December. In January 1915, however, they were defeated by Jacobus van Deventer; Kemp was taken prisoner but the wily Maritz

escaped to Angola.

The rebellion had failed but at some cost. At the end of 1914 rebel forces under Jopie Fourie and J J Pienaar had inflicted heavy casualties in two actions, but on 15 December nearly all were captured. Fourie had unwisely omitted to resign his commission in the Active Citizen Force and had fired under a flag of truce; he was therefore sentenced to death by court martial. His execution on 20 December was entirely legal but he was rapidly elevated to the status of martyr, and Smuts was held responsible for his death in nationalist circles. Accusations about the execution of Jopie Fourie pursued Smuts to his grave, and it is hard not to argue that clemency might have been the wiser course.

In essence the 1914 Rebellion was a domestic affair, with only 300 deaths on both sides. In retrospect it was seen as an internal squabble among Afrikaners that was put down largely by Afrikaners, with no recourse to the British for help. Apart from the shooting of Fourie the rebels were punished by fines and short terms of imprisonment; even Kemp, a ringleader, received seven years in prison and a £1000 fine, while de Wet got six years' imprisonment and was fined £2000. By 1916 all were released.

Left: General Christiaan de Wet took to the field once more in the Rebellion but his depleted force was hunted down by troops in cars. He surrendered to Botha near Vryburg on 1 December 1914.

Below: De Wet was sentenced to six years in prison and a fine of £2000, but he was released in 1916.

Above: General Christiaan Beyers, a leading light in the 1914 Rebellion. He died while trying to cross the Vaal River on horseback.

Left: Boer commandos arriving in Johannesburg in October 1914 to deal with the Rebellion. It was the last time the burghers answered the traditional call.

JAN CHRISTIAAN SMUTS

Jan Christiaan Smuts was born in 1870 near Riebeek West in the Cape Colony, and soon demonstrated an outstanding intellectual ability that was to put him head and shoulders above his contemporaries for the rest of his life.

After graduating with a Double First in Law at Christ's College, Cambridge, he practised at the Cape Bar until disillusionment with Rhodes and outrage at the Jameson Raid confirmed his fundamental sympathies with Afrikaner independence. He went north to the Transvaal, where President Kruger recognised his abilities by appointing him State Attorney in 1897.

The young State Attorney enjoyed his new responsibilities. He brought the 'Zarps' (the Transvaal police, known as such from their *Zuid Afrikaansche Republiek* shoulder-flashes) under tighter control, in an effort to reduce the fears of the Uitlanders. He was less successful in rooting out corruption, for the South African Republic relied heavily on the network of concessions and monopolies granted to foreign contractors, but he earned a reputation as a high-principled administrator.

With single-minded energy Smuts threw himself into the war, and showed his skill by leading a successful attack on the Cape Colony in 1901, but when he saw the situation was hopeless he supported Botha's efforts to bring the fighting to an end. As one of the architects of the Union he was rewarded with Cabinet rank in 1910, but his critics complained about his boundless ambition. Often he held several portfolios simultaneously, and he did not hesitate to use military force in support of the civil power during the 1913 strike; his use of Imperial troops incurred further odium among his critics. In the railway strike the following year he declared martial law, but this time he had sufficient South African forces to enable him to act without calling in Imperial units. This time the strike was crushed with the loss of only two lives. Without resorting to the tiresome delay of a trial Smuts deported nine foreign-born union leaders to Europe, earning him the enmity of the labour movement.

The First World War pushed Smuts to the centre of the world stage. Ironically his period of overall command in East Africa in 1916-17 revealed his shortcomings as a military man. As his shrewd Chief of Intelligence Captain Meinertzhagen put it. 'Smuts was not an astute soldier; a brilliant statesman and politician, but no soldier.' The British Government, however, was more interested in his intellect than his military record, and he joined the British War Cabinet early in 1917. It was his recommendation that led to the establishment of the Royal Air Force in 1918, and in 1919 he was a delegate to the Paris Peace Conference. Smuts fought in vain for a just (and enforceable) peace for Germany, predicting correctly that a harsh settlement would last only as long as it took Germany to recover from the effects of the war.

In South Africa his international role as a statesman has been overshadowed by his controversial domestic political career. He succeeded Botha as premier but was defeated in

Left: Smuts and the 1921 Union Cabinet, which included N J de Wet, Deneys Reitz, Patrick Duncan, J W Jagger, Henrik Mentz, Sir Thomas Watt, F S Malan, Sir Thomas Smartt and H Burton.

Left: Jan Smuts in the field as a commandant during the Anglo-Boer War.

Right: Smuts as a Field Marshal in the Second World War. While Hofmeyr ran the country virtually single handed Smuts was free to concentrate on the war and foreign affairs.

1924. Thereafter he fought in harness with Hertzog and the Nationalists until he was returned to office in 1939, at the age of 69. Once again world events seemed to fulfil Smuts' dream of a wider role for South Africa as a dominion of the British Empire, with Afrikaners and English-speakers living happily together. This dream, however, was founded on false assumptions. Nationalist sentiment was opposed to a second expensive 'British' war, and extreme right-wing elements worked actively to support Germany and sabotage South Africa's war effort, thus forcing Smuts to resort to repressive measures to control the unrest.

Like Churchill, Smuts had to endure the humiliation of leading his country to victory only to be turned out of office by a disgruntled post-war generation looking for a 'new deal'. He had failed to convince sufficient of his countrymen to work for his notion of a wider role for South Africa. His was a complex and subtle personality which was never fully understood by his contemporaries. Today his work seems largely forgotten in South Africa, but he is undeniably the only South African statesman to achieve international stature. Smuts' legacy ranges from the creation of the Union of South Africa to the foundation of the UN; and although both have their critics the world would be very different without them.

Above: Smuts with Winston Churchill at the British Embassy in Cairo in August 1942. On Churchill's left are Generals Sir Claude Auchinleck and Sir Archibald Wavell.

Left: Smuts in 1941, wearing UDF uniform.

THE FIRST WORLD WAR
THE CONQUEST OF SOUTH WEST AFRICA

Despite the rumours of rebellion the Union Government was not put off its plans to neutralise the German forces in South West Africa. On 1 September 1914 a force under Brigadier-General Lukin landed at Port Nolloth, and 17 days later another force landed at Luderitz Bay, securing a bridgehead for future operations. But inevitably the outbreak of the rebellion in October made it impossible to take the offensive and it was not until May 1915 that enough troops could be spared. Then Louis Botha moved with 40,000 men under his command.

At the time the South West Africa operations were hailed as a brilliant coup, and proof that the rebellion had been firmly suppressed. But clearly the 9000 German defenders stood little chance. The British Government had in fact put pressure on the South African Government to move against South West Africa, on the grounds that German radio stations on the coast were relaying information about shipping to German warships. Botha had little option but to agree to invade, for London made it clear that Imperial troops would be used should he refuse. It must also have been clear that South Africa would have a good claim to the territory when the spoils were divided after the war was over.

The main objective, neutralising the radio stations at Swakopmund and Luderitz Bay had already been achieved when troops landed in August but now it was necessary to pacify the whole country. Botha led the main column from Swakopmund, striking eastwards to attack Windhoek, while three smaller columns commanded by Smuts were to strike, one east from Luderitz Bay and two north from the South African

Above: Botha and Smuts in July 1919, on their return from the Versailles Peace Conference.

Left: A train crosses the Orange River, carrying supplies for the South West Africa campaign.

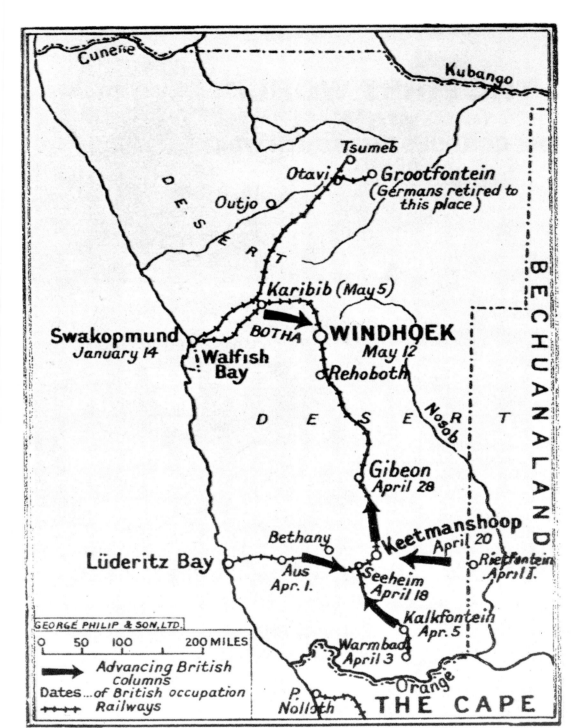

Below: South African troops halt on the march. The terrain was more of an enemy than the Germans, who were heavily outnumbered.

border. These three columns were to unite at Keetmanshoop and then continue to march north. Botha and Smuts knew from their own experience as guerrilla leaders what mischief could be done by seasoned troops left at large.

Serious operations did not get under way until April 1915. Many delays were caused by Afrikaans- and English-speaking officers arguing with each other, and by inefficiency (or dishonesty, some said) in the Remounts and Transport Service. The German Commander-in-Chief General von Heydebreck prudently withdrew into the interior, leaving Smuts' columns to struggle through the waterless desert. On 25 April his columns united as planned and fell upon the Germans at Gibeon. Heavy losses were inflicted, but Smuts' troops failed to trap the main German force.

On 6 May Botha took Karibib and within a fortnight he had occupied Windhoek. The German Governor Seitz tried to negotiate a ceasefire; each side would retain the ground occupied at the time, and settlement would have to await the peace con-

ference. The offer was rejected by the South Africans who were in a very strong position, despite the presence of 4000 German troops in the northern part of the country. Botha needed time to regroup and acquire fresh mounts, and was not able to renew the offensive until early June, but as soon as his troops were ready he set off once more. The refreshed troops made an astounding march, covering 120 miles in a single week, and the last German forces under Franke surrendered at Tsumeb on 9 July 1915.

The cost in financial terms had been heavy, and by any standards the campaign was extravagant in the numbers of troops deployed, although it had been cheap in lives. Out of a final total of 50,000 troops only 113 had been killed and 311 wounded. The Union Defence Force had acquitted itself well in its first 'overseas' campaign, and the victory went some way towards distracting attention from the rebellion. It also secured for South Africa virtually certain control over the future of South West Africa.

Above: Mounted troops near Upington, close to the border with German South West Africa.

Left: General Botha negotiating an armistice with Dr Seitz, the Governor of German South West Africa. The German surrender was signed at Korab on 9 July 1915.

THE FIRST WORLD WAR
FIGHTING LETTOW-VORBECK

It is ironic that South Africans found their most formidable foe to be a master of guerrilla warfare and a regular soldier commanding mainly black troops. The East African campaign lasted over two-and-a-half years and required the services of 60,000 South African troops, and when the Armistice came the Germans were still at large.

The British campaign in East Africa in 1914-15 had suffered many disasters and setbacks, so that an offer of South African help proved particularly welcome. In August 1915 General van Deventer arrived to advise on how best to co-operate and integrate the South African reinforcements; by the end of the year troops had arrived, and this put new heart into the campaign.

Smuts had been offered the command in November; at first he refused because of domestic political worries, but when it was re-offered he accepted, and he arrived in Nairobi in February 1916. Roles were reversed, as this time Smuts had numerous mediocre British senior officers under his command, whereas the Germans were led by General Paul von Lettow-Vorbeck, a brilliant guerrilla fighter.

In spite of his difficulties Smuts achieved important suc-

cesses before the rainy season brought campaigning to an end in March 1916. He had removed the threat to the Kenya-Uganda Railway, and Imperial forces had at last begun to fight on German territory.

When the next phase began in October, Smuts found that his worst enemy was the climate. He was later to write that between October and December it had been necessary to evacuate 12-15,000 sick soldiers, most of whom were suffering from malaria. Time was to show that the native black askari was the only soldier suited to East African conditions, so that both sides leaned more and more heavily on black troops.

Although Smuts showed much originality and energy he did not succeed in his main aim of neutralising Lettow-Vorbeck. When he left East Africa in January 1917 to represent South Africa at the Imperial Defence Conference Smuts claimed that the campaign was over, and that all that remained to be done was for the remnants of the German force to be swept up. The greater part of German East Africa was now in British hands but the hunt for Lettow-Vorbeck would last another 20 months, making nonsense of Smuts' claim. While caution saved battle casualties — Smuts had no intention of

being labelled 'Butcher Smuts' back home — his Fabian tactics meant that the number of deaths from sickness, rather than action, multiplied.

On 25 November 1917 Lettow-Vorbeck crossed into Portuguese East Africa. His force now comprised only 300 Germans, 1700 askaris and 3000 porters, and against him the British had ranged more men than Roberts had required in 1900. The task confronting General van Deventer was complicated by the thick bush. His objectives were to prevent the Germans from slipping back into German East Africa and to head off any attempt to invade Nyasaland. But in spite of all his efforts the Germans retained the initiative. Time and again forces were held up by skilful rearguard actions, an uncomfortable reminder that the successes of the Anglo-Boer War could not entirely be credited to divine intervention: small fast-moving forces are often able to outwit slower-moving superior forces. Lettow-Vorbeck was still fighting two days after the Armistice, which he first heard about in a telegram from Jacobus van Deventer:

. . . Clause 17 of armistice signed by German government provides for unconditional surrender of all German forces operating in East Africa within one month from November 11. My conditions are, first, hand over all prisoners in your hands, second, bring your forces to Abercorn without delay, third, hand over all your arms to my representative at Abercorn. I will, however, allow you and your officers and European ranks to retain their arms for the present in consideration of the gallant fight which you have made, provided that you bring your force to Abercorn without delay.

It was a fitting and chivalrous end to a war not otherwise distinguished for its humanity. Lettow-Vorbeck surrendered at the head of his troops and was granted full military honours. Over 1500 South African troops had died during the campaign, tied down in a secondary theatre of war in which their fighting qualities were, if not wasted, used to less than full effect. Elsewhere, however, South African troops were proving their fighting qualities.

Above left: General Paul von Lettow-Vorbeck led the South African forces a dance through East Africa. He surrendered with the honours of war two days after the Armistice in November 1918.

Left: South African troops entering Nairobi at the end of 1915.

THE FIRST WORLD WAR
DELVILLE WOOD

Although the epic of Delville Wood lives on in South African history as the only memorable action in the European theatre, a 6000-strong contingent was sent to England as early as December 1915. It was, however, immediately re-routed to Egypt to defend the Suez Canal against a Turkish offensive, and it was later used against the Senussi in the Western Desert.

In April 1916 the 1st South African Brigade, still under the command of Brigadier-General H T Lukin, finally reached France, where it became part of the 9th Division. The Brigade had first seen service in the Battle of the Somme, and on 13 July 1916 it received orders to take the village of Longueval as well as Delville Wood on the far side; the wood would help defend a recently captured salient from machine-gun and artillery fire.

When final orders were given for the assault at first light on 15 July three battalions moved out in open order, but the wood proved so thick that it was impossible to reach open ground without incurring heavy casualties. Part of the village, fortified with deep dugouts and stone pillboxes armed with machine-guns, was still in enemy hands. The advance was met by a heavy German counter-attack towards the middle of the

day, but was repulsed with the loss of nearly all 2/107th Reserve Regiment's officers. Later during the day and well into the night there were further attacks, some with flame-throwers and others accompanied by massive artillery bombardments, but the defenders held on. Relief of the Brigade could not be effected for three days, but the last remnants were not extracted until late on 20 July. When the roll was called only 29 officers and 751 other ranks were present. Since 1 July the South Africans had suffered 1080 killed or missing and 1735 wounded; out of 120 officers 23 were dead, 15 taken prisoner and 74 wounded. Marshal Foch was to write, 'The heroic dead of South Africa, whether Dutch or British by origin,

France will never forget what she owes them.'

In retrospect Delville Wood has merged into the vast blood bath of the Somme, but insofar as that four-month-long holocaust was a victory in the war of attrition against the German Army, the heroic defence of that strategically significant piece of the battlefield was important.

After resting and receiving fresh drafts the Brigade took part in the 1917 offensive to dislodge the Germans from Belgium. Under Lukin, now a Major-General, it fought in the titanic Third Battle of Ypres in September 1917. In March 1918 the Brigade suffered heavy casualties stemming the German offensive and it went on to fight at Marrières Wood and again

Far left: Troops digging a communication trench through Delville Wood after the battle.

Left: Artist's impression of the Battle of Delville Wood, which the South African Brigade defended for nearly three weeks.

at Messines Ridge in May. By the last months of the war the Brigade could barely muster the equivalent of a battalion.

The contribution of blacks to the war is usually ignored. Although the South African Government had declined an offer of black, Coloured and Indian recruits for the Army, use was made of all black groups for ancillary services. Coloureds were used for a short while as scouts in South West Africa, and a Cape Corps was finally allowed to bear arms in East Africa. Indians also served in that campaign, but as stretcher-bearers.

With considerable reluctance permission was given to recruit a South African Native Labour Contingent (SANLC) to provide a labour force in France, where trained (white) man-power was needed in the trenches. Although there was under-standable reluctance to join, eventually some 21,000 SANLC were sent to France, where their capacity for hard work earned them praise. But it was laid down that they must be housed in segregated compounds, lest they return to South Africa with radical ideas about freedom and the lack of a colour bar.

Despite their co-operation the blacks did not receive any re-ward for their loyalty. The clear evidence from East Africa that black soldiers were more resistant to disease was ignored, in spite of warnings from Smuts and other military observers.

THE RAND REBELLION

The war had caused inflation, and inevitably the black community suffered worse than most. Black miners had gone on limited strike and boycotted shops from late 1915 until mid-1918, while white miners looked to job restriction to protect their position in the post-war world.

At the end of the war there was a short-lived boom, but a fall in the price of gold ushered in another round of cost-cutting by employers. At the end of 1921 the Chamber of Mines warned its workers that it would cut the wages of the highest-paid white workers, that reservation of specific jobs to whites would be abolished, and that lower-paid blacks would be allowed to perform some semi-skilled jobs.

What followed was an ugly confrontation between the Government and organised white labour. Many interested parties tried to make capital out of the dispute; Communists looked for a way to undermine capitalism, while Nationalists hoped to establish an Afrikaans-speaking *Mynwerkersbond* to bring the mines away from what they saw as foreign control. Anarchy was in the air, with appeals being made to the Active Citizen Force to disobey the call-up, and miners forming 'commandos' to resist strike-breaking.

tion. A General Strike was proclaimed on 7 March, and two days later Smuts mobilised the Active Citizen Force and declared martial law.

The fighting that followed lasted only eight days but it was at times bitter. In Brakpan mine officials and police were killed brutally, and both the Imperial Light Horse and the Transvaal Scottish suffered losses in clashes. To break the strikers' hold on areas it proved necessary to call up artillery and aircraft. A full casualty list was never made available, but official statistics claimed that 43 troops, 86 policemen and 81 civilians were killed, while 133 troops, 86 policemen and 315 civilians were injured. The civilian casualties included an estimated 39 'revolutionaries' killed. Some 5000 were arrested, of whom 1000 were brought to trial; 18 were sentenced to death but only four ringleaders were hanged.

In the aftermath many accusations were bandied about, but there seems little doubt that a number of strikers were shot 'while trying to escape'. Under the hastily enacted Indemnity

Left: Mounted police riding out to confront the strikers.

Above right: A union leader tries to disperse strikers gathered outside a courthouse in which miners are on trial.

Right: Uneasy peace reigns as mounted police confront strikers outside the Johannesburg General Post Office.

The first clash occurred on 27 February 1922 when police clashed with miners at Angelo. There was no shooting but several arrests were made. Next day the police fired on a large body moving on Boksburg Gaol, killing three strikers. At first the Government tried to stay aloof, 'to draw a ring around both parties', as Smuts put it. In fact Smuts had already tried to negotiate between the Chamber of Mines and the unions, but neither party was in a mood for compromise.

An 'Augmented Executive' was formed to co-ordinate the various unions and workers out on strike but by the end of February effective leadership was in the hands of the more militant Council of Action, which favoured direct confronta-

and Trial of Offenders Bill special courts were set up to try all those accused of murder, whereas all accused of lesser offences were tried by judge and jury.

The 1922 strikers showed no solidarity with black mineworkers. The Mineworkers' Union had come out on strike with the main purpose of maintaining the colour bar and, with no sense of irony, the Fordsburg Commando fought under the slogan, 'Workers of the World Unite and Fight for a White South Africa' – socialist ideas at their most pragmatic.

Smuts was denounced by the Nationalists for allegedly allowing the strike to develop, but the charges did not stick. Unfortunately for him, his tough handling of the 1914 Rebellion and the 1913-14 strikes made it easy to portray him as insensitive; but it was also to count heavily against him in the 1924 General Election.

RURAL DEPRESSION

Internal rivalries were as dangerous as ever after the First World War, and the war had done nothing to help. The alienation of labour and capital increased and there was still no true reconciliation between Afrikaner and Briton. Nor had the blacks any reason to hope for improvement. What was being created remorselessly was a pecking order in which English-speaking whites took precedence over Afrikaans-speakers, who in turn took precedence over blacks. Neither Botha nor Smuts had done anything to reverse this trend, preferring to suppress black discontent rather than tamper with its root causes.

By 1922 an estimated half of the mineworkers on the Rand were Afrikaners. Since before the Anglo-Boer War there had been a steady growth of 'poor whites' as impoverished farmers drifted to the towns in search of work. A poor white could be defined as someone unable to find a proper means of livelihood for himself or to obtain it for his children. To a proud people who were brought up on traditions of the *lekker lewe* and who felt themselves to be caught up in the long struggle to escape from British rule, it was even more humiliating to sink to a level of subsistence. It was not surprising, therefore, that for the Afrikaners preserving their position relative to the black population transcended all other ambitions.

Many urban Afrikaners turned to the Labour Party, which brought them into contact with English workers and the world of organised labour and trade unions. However, the Labour Party never succeeded in creating a bilingual constituency; its leader Colonel Frank Cresswell had forfeited the support of most rural Afrikaners by his support for the war in 1914.

In 1924 the Nationalist Party came to power under Hertzog, largely with the help of the Labour Party. His republican wing had to play down its long-term aims to keep the Labour members of the electoral pact happy, but that did not prevent Hert-

Above: Harvesting pawpaws. The post-war slump hit the rural economy hard, and a short-lived boom was followed by the Great Depression at the end of the 1920s.

Left: White diamond miners at work in the Kimberley Mine.

Right: Sugar was the staple crop of Natal.

Above: Cotton picking by black women and children.

Right: Dr Daniel François Malan won the 1948 General Election on a pledge to enforce *apartheid*.

zog from pursuing his broad aim of restoring the position of the Afrikaner nation. In 1925 the Constitution was amended to admit Afrikaans as an official language rather than High Dutch, and to give it full equality with English. Bilingualism became mandatory throughout the civil service, offering a major route of advancement to comparatively poor Afrikaners.

An attempt was made to get rid of the hated Union flag, but when Dr D F Malan, Minister of the Interior, Education and Public Health, proposed a new 'neutral' flag he caused uproar. English-speakers saw (correctly) in Malan's proposals for a flag a symbolic first step towards secession from the Empire and the re-creation of an Afrikaner republic. After nearly three years a compromise was finally reached, with a new national flag incorporating the old Free State and Transvaal republican flags as well as the Union flag. To symbolise the Union's association with the Empire the Union flag was to be flown alongside the national flag on government buildings.

Hertzog was fortunate to take office at a time when the economy was buoyant. The mining industry had recovered, manufacturing industry was prosperous and agricultural prices had risen. Customs tariffs were imposed in 1925 to encourage secondary industry, and in 1928 the Iron and Steel Industrial Corporation (ISCOR) was established as a public utility.

Hertzog and his Labour allies were determined to free the country from the economic dominance of Britain. However quaint it may seem in the last quarter of the century, many people believed that gold was a diminishing asset. It therefore became an urgent priority to industrialise the country to compensate for the eventual loss of gold revenue. Other priorities

were the need to provide employment for poor whites, to stop cheap black labour from destroying white skilled employment, and to check the outflow of foreign exchange.

Under the guise of ensuring the survival of 'civilised labour at civilised rates' the Pact Government wanted preference given to whites over blacks in employment, and at higher wages. The Mines and Works Amendment Act of 1926 restored several colour bar regulations which had previously been invalidated in the courts. Dr Malan had already proposed an Areas Reservation and Immigration and Registration Bill to secure segregation of the Indian community in housing and employment.

The Indian community was able to marshal strong support for their opposition. Gone were the days of passive resistance; instead the South African Indian Council sought help from India and Britain. At the end of 1926 the first round-table conference was arranged between the South African and Indian Governments. The purpose was to look at ways of repatriating Indians and to improve the lot of those Indians who wished to stay. Major concessions won were the South African Government's agreement to withdraw the offending Areas Reservation legislation, and a promise to promote the 'upliftment' of the Indian community.

THE RESURGENCE OF AFRIKANERDOM

Above: Dr Malan's platform for the 1948 election played down the plans for a republic, thereby securing a decisive share of the moderate Afrikaner vote.

Left: General Hertzog found himself increasingly alienated from mainstream Nationalism. He died embittered and disillusioned.

At the 1926 Imperial Conference in London Arthur Balfour clearly defined the position of South Africa and the other Dominions: equal status with Great Britain within the Empire. All the dominions were 'autonomous communities within the British Empire, equal in status, in no way subordinate one to another in any respect of their domestic or external affairs . . .'. As direct proof of this assertion Hertzog created a new portfolio for himself, the Department of External Affairs. As Minister of Native Affairs he also took another step down the road towards apartheid. In July 1926 he tabled three 'native' bills. The Union Native Council Bill proposed a deliberative council with 50 African members, 35 of them elected. The Representation of Natives in Parliament Bill proposed to remove African voters from the common roll in the Cape, and in return to provide all Africans with seven white representatives in the House of Assembly, with power to vote only on measures affecting Africans. The third measure, the Natives Land Act (Amendment) Bill would reduce the area allocated to Africans in the 1913 Act by releasing land for competitive purchase by whites and blacks. In addition to these three bills Hertzog also tabled a Coloured Persons Rights Bill which proposed extending political rights to Coloureds outside the Cape.

The bills failed to win support, even after two years of deliberation by a select committee, and did not get into the statute book for another ten years. The effect on black opinion was to increase their disillusionment with Hertzog. Ironically the newly renamed African National Congress (formerly the SANNC) and the Industrial and Commercial Workers Union (ICU) had welcomed the Nationalist victory, hoping that it would bring in changes. However the 'native' bills threatened to take away the few rights of the tiny black middle class, from whose ranks the leaders of the ANC and ICU were drawn.

The ANC was as a result turned from a cautious, moderate organisation into a radical force. Some of its leaders forged links with the Communist Party, and under Joseph Gumede the ANC started to turn itself into a mass organisation. The ICU was even more successful at turning itself into a mass movement, targeting both rural and urban blacks and Coloureds. By 1927 it had recruited an estimated 100,000 members. But the union soon went into decline, harassed by the State and the employers but largely destroyed by its own internal squabbles. The ANC too, lost ground under pressure from the Government, and replaced the radical Gumede with the moderate Pixley Seme as president.

In the 1929 General Election the colour question was for the first time a dominant issue. Hertzog tried to present himself and his party as the only true champions of the whites, labelling Smuts and his South Africa Party as advocates of racial equality – a preposterous charge but good enough to secure a Nationalist victory.

Hertzog hoped to continue along the same path now that he had an outright majority but he reckoned without the Great Depression. South Africa clung to the mythical protection of the gold standard, and refused to follow Britain when she

abandoned it in 1931. For two long years the economy suffered, with the South African pound over-valued at nearly twice that of the Australian pound. Sanity finally prevailed when the former Minister of Justice Tielman Roos made a dramatic intervention, launching an appeal for a national (coalition) government. As in Britain in 1931 the abandonment of the gold standard resulted in an immediate improvement in the economy, and Smuts felt confident enough to propose a coalition to Hertzog.

The new Coalition Government became a reality in March 1933, with Smuts as Deputy Prime Minister and Minister of Justice. The Cabinet contained six Nationalists and six members of the South African Party; the former Labour members were dropped. The next step was to fuse the two parties, and in June 1934 Hertzog published his Programme of Principles. When the new United Party was launched in December, Dr Daniel Malan and his followers left to form the *Gesuiwerde* or Purified National Party, while Colonel Stallard and six English-speaking MPs left to form the Dominion Party.

Although the so-called Fusion Government lacked cohesion the general improvement in the economy papered over the cracks in party unity. A gold boom triggered off a general upsurge of growth throughout the economy, increasing national income from £234.7 million in 1932-33 to £394.8 million in 1938-39, an increase of 68.2 per cent.

Left: The SA Communist Party published the *South African Worker* until it was suppressed.

Below: Delegates to the 1930 African National Congress in Bloemfontein.

THE SECOND WORLD WAR
SOUTH AFRICA GOES TO WAR AGAIN

The news that Great Britain had declared war on Germany on 3 September 1939 once again split the country, but this time there was to be no overt act of rebellion. Hertzog tried to keep South Africa neutral, hoping that the Purified National Party would support him, while Smuts predictably proposed that South Africa should follow the British.

In the debate that followed Hertzog made a tactical error when, in the name of South African independence, he compared Hitler's 'struggle for liberty' with his own; Smuts won the day with the argument that it would be impossible to reconcile neutrality with Commonwealth obligations. When the Governor-General refused Hertzog's request to dissolve Parliament Hertzog resigned, allowing Smuts to form a new government.

While the country as a whole supported Smuts (some 55 per cent of the Army volunteers were Afrikaners) the right-wing politicians were deeply divided. Malan persuaded Hertzog not to form a new party, and instead his supporters joined a new *Herenigde Nasionale* or *Volksparty* (Reunited National or People's Party). The Nationalists were having trouble with what had originally been their 'cultural' wing, the *Ossewabrandwag* (Oxwagon Sentinel) movement. With the country at war the 'OB', as it was commonly known, became more militant; its *Stormjaers* (shock troops) started to ape Nazi stormtroopers, carrying out acts of sabotage and assaulting soldiers in uniform. Membership of the OB grew at an alarming pace, and by 1941 it was officially estimated that the OB numbered between 300,000 and 400,000.

Above: A portrait of Smuts, painted by Sir William Nicholson.

Far left: Recruiting drivers for the Cape Corps, a successful wartime expedient. Some 120,000 black and coloured personnel served with the armed forces, but only as labourers and drivers.

Left: Some of Hertzog's ministers made no secret of their admiration for Nazi Germany. Oswald Pirow, the Defence Minister, met Ribbentrop (centre) during a visit to Berlin in November 1938.

Smuts had no alternative but to crack down hard on pro-Nazi elements, and several Nationalist luminaries, including future Prime Minister B J Vorster, were interned. A former heavyweight boxing champion Robey Leibrandt was put ashore from a German submarine to set up a sabotage network, but was quickly arrested. Smuts, perhaps remembering the damage he had suffered over the years for executing Jopie Fourie, merely put the Nazi saboteur behind bars.

The activities of the OB embarrassed Malan and his party. In 1942 he banned National Party officials from joining the organisation, and in 1944 even proposed extending the ban to all party members. The Special Branch crackdown also weakened the OB but the movement's decline was undoubtedly linked to a realisation that Nazi Germany was not going to win the war. By 1943 the OB was no more than a minor irritant in South African political life.

Hertzog, for all his work to protect the position of Afrikaners, clung to an ideal of a nation united but independent of

British control. At the National Party Congress in the Free State in November 1940 his plans to protect the rights of English-speakers were rejected. He resigned in protest, leaving the high ground to extremists whose views he could not stomach. He was also humiliated at the Transvaal Congress a month later, when the party voted to exclude Jews and voted down Hertzog's proposal for a republic based on consensus between the white races. Hertzog and N C Havenga resigned their parliamentary seats in December 1940 to form the Afrikaner Party, but the new organisation failed to become more than a splinter group. Hertzog's remarkable political career had spanned some 45 years and in many respects matched that of his arch-rival Smuts. But he had none of Smuts' interest in world affairs. His unique role as the champion of the Afrikaner people had been taken from him by Malan and a new breed of nationalists.

Right: Recruits flock to the colours. Restrictions on service outside the Union were lifted in 1940, and after 1943 troops could volunteer to fight outside Africa.

Below: The Transvaal Scottish preparing to embark on a troopship in August 1940.

THE SECOND WORLD WAR
'UP NORTH'

The Defence Act limited the UDF's (Union Defence Force) operational area to South Africa (however loosely defined) but in 1940 this provision was relaxed to allow soldiers to serve anywhere in Africa. South Africans (mostly volunteers), now wearing the distinctive 'red tab' shoulder-flash, began fighting in East Africa, Madagascar and North Africa. In 1943 Parliament removed the 'Africa Only' regulation, so that troops were permitted to volunteer for service in Sicily and Italy.

Unlike the previous conflict in the region during the First World War, the East African campaign was virtually an all-South African effort from the start. The first decisive engagement for South African troops took place at El Wak when they defeated the Italians in 1940; South African troops were also the most important element in the defeat of the Duke of Aosta's army at Amba Alagi the following year. Thousands of Italian PoWs were sent back to South Africa, where many were paroled to work as farm labourers. The price of destroying Italian military power in Eritrea and Abyssinia was not high: 73 South African troops killed and 197 wounded.

Above: South African troops in their distinctive pith helmets, in a road convoy in East Africa in July 1940.

Left: Map reading in the East African bush.

Left: Motorised infantry 'debussing' in the Libyan Desert.

Right: A minesweeper converted from a whalecatcher, lying in Alexandria. Many trawlers and whalers served as minesweepers and escorts, but from 1944 regular warships became available from the Royal Navy.

Below: Some of the thousands of South African PoWs taken at the fall of Tobruk in June 1942.

Bottom: Drafting daily orders during the East African campaign.

South African forces also took part in the capture of Madagascar in 1942 to forestall a possible Japanese invasion, but the major campaign was in North Africa. By the beginning of March 1941 the presence in the Middle East theatre of the Afrika Korps had tilted the balance against the British, Australian and New Zealand forces, and the call went out for South African reinforcements. In all, two divisions were sent to North Africa.

The desert was harsh, with extremes of heat and cold. Campaigning presented a challenge to human endurance, and the terrain dictated a totally new type of warfare. During the 'Crusader' offensive in November 1941 the 1st SA Division received orders to attack enemy armour and infantry in the vicinity of Sidi Rezegh. On 25 November a German tank force attacked and overran 5th Brigade's position. 1st Brigade also engaged German armour and inflicted heavy loss before withdrawing safely. The battle demonstrated that infantry were not able to defend themselves against armour unless well-placed in a good defensive position.

The fall of the fortress of Tobruk resulted in the capture of nearly 11,000 South Africans and 14,000 British and Indians. The defeat rankled all the more because Australians had held Tobruk successfully the year before. On paper Major General Klopper had stronger forces than his predecessor but in fact the Guards Brigade was badly under-strength through casualties, the artillery was short of transport and ammuniton, and only obsolescent tanks were available.

On 20 June 1942 the perimeter was attacked by two German armoured divisions, with a motorised division, an Italian armoured division and three Italian infantry divisions in sup-

port. Heavy air attacks paralysed the defenders, and the whole fortress was overrun within eight hours. Klopper proposed a mass breakout during the night but most of his transport had been destroyed. After holding a shortened perimeter during the night he ordered his forces to lay down their arms next day. Two South African divisions later took part in the two battles of El Alamein. In the October battle the artillery fired 62,000 rounds, and South African armoured cars were prominent among the first Eighth Army units to re-enter Tobruk on 12 November.

While the major fighting was on land the two other services, the South African Navy (SAN) and the South African Air Force (SAAF), also played their part in the Allied victory. The Sea-

ward Defence Force, known jocularly as the 'Seaweed Defence Force', was largely improvised from whalecatchers and trawlers to provide coastal escort in the Mediterranean. An even more useful contribution was the salvage ship *Gamtoos*, which helped to clear harbours of sunken shipping.

Both the SAN and the SAAF received modern equipment from Britain as ships and aircraft became available. In 1944-45 the Royal Navy transferred three new anti-submarine frigates, while the SAAF progressed from a force of obsolete biplanes to a modern force of fighters and bombers. While the SAAF had achieved remarkable successes in East Africa, in the Western Desert SAAF pilots showed that they could hold their own against the Luftwaffe's best.

THE SECOND WORLD WAR
FIGHTING IN ITALY

Above: Bren gun carriers of the Imperial Light Horse (Kimberley Regiment) advancing through the narrow streets of Florence.

Left: Sherman tanks of the 6th South African Armoured Division captured Orvieto on 14 June 1944 during the advance beyond Rome.

The Allied victory in North Africa in May 1943 released forces for an offensive against Italy, and the opportunity was taken to form a 6th South African Armoured Division. Although there was some delay in finding volunteers to serve outside Africa this formation finally emerged as the most powerful South African unit fielded in 1939-45.

The division arrived at Taranto in April 1944. Conditions in North Africa had been very different from the mountainous terrain in Italy, but the division gave a good account of itself in the assault on Monte Cassino. The skilful German defence of Italy frustrated any hope that the country would prove the 'soft underbelly of the Axis' and fighting continued right up to May 1945. The 6th SA Armoured Division was in action until the end of April 1945, when the Allied command stopped the advance. South African casualties in the whole Italian campaign amounted to 753 dead and 4416 wounded.

As in 1914-18 the black community played a major part but they were allowed to serve only in auxiliary roles. The Government talked the British out of arming Bechuana and Basuto recruits with anything more lethal than knobkerries and assegais, nor was there any question of South African blacks, Coloureds and Indians serving in any capacity other than as labourers or drivers. In all about 120,000 blacks served with the South African forces on all their campaigns.

Black political organisations took a largely conciliatory line on supporting the war effort, although many blacks were to question the enormous gap between the Allies' claim that they were fighting for universal freedom, and the realities the black population experienced of their own position. In 1943 the ANC's annual conference drew attention to the specific promises contained in the Atlantic Charter and reached the conclusion that they implied full citizenship rights for blacks.

Despite all the achievements of its soldiers, South Africa's outstanding contribution to the Second World War was achieving a high industrial output. To raise, train and equip three divisions required an immense effort, most of it using local resources. To help relieve the strain on war production in beleaguered Britain, South African factories took up production of standard small arms, munitions and artillery. Even armoured cars were designed and built, and the country pro-

vided excellent training facilities. Many wounded Allied soldiers were sent south to convalesce, a further benefit to the total war effort. In all, some 200,000 South Africans served with the armed forces, of whom about 9000 were killed.

The expansion of the economy to meet war demands created a boom which lasted until the end of the war in 1945; but it also created an insatiable demand for labour which accelerated the process of urbanising both Afrikaners and blacks. On the credit side the expansion generated many advances in technology and speeded the adoption of modern industrial production methods. The drift from the countryside to the towns exacerbated social tensions, however, and created problems which today are very serious. The war also laid the foundations of the formidable military machine that exists today.

Above: The advance on Rome saw heavy fighting, but the Eternal City was spared bombardment. Allied troops occupied the city with no resistance.

Right: Shermans of the Special Service Battalion (SSB), part of 6th SA Armoured Division, crossed the River Arno at Empoli.

Left: 6th SA Armoured Division captured Florence on 8 August 1944, entering through the ancient Porta Romana.

PEACE AND REACTION

Left: Police using their batons on striking mineworkers. The 1946 strike put ten mines out of action and cut gold production in many others.

Right: For most urban blacks the only weapon against rising bus fares was a boycott. The police retaliated by impounding unlicensed taxis.

Below right: For those who could not afford taxis a bus boycott meant a long walk to work.

Below: The war economy created a huge demand for skilled white and unskilled black labour. It also created massive social problems which have not yet been solved.

The Government was determined not to repeat the mistakes made after the First World War, when boom had rapidly given way to slump. As early as 1940 the Industrial Development Corporation had been set up to promote new industries and Dr J H van Eck's Social and Economic Planning Council had looked at ways of modernising the economy. Pressures of war production helped, and the lack of imported consumer goods was a spur to local manufacturers.

The greatest single social problem was the increasing drift of black people into the cities. Efforts to improve agricultural efficiency pre-war merely exacerbated the problems. Mechanisation on the farms improved yields but farmers still complained about the shortage of black labourers, who left the land to look for work in the cities.

The war economy demanded labour on an unprecedented scale, to the point where influx control was relaxed and the possibility was discussed of revising the pass laws, whereby blacks were required to carry identification documents at all times. But there was little prosperity to be found in the cities. Urban conditions were bad, with wages failing to match high rents and high food and transport costs. The huge influx into urban areas increased the strain on already meagre services and produced an acute shortage of housing.

By 1945 it was clear that the policy of treating Africans as 'temporary sojourners' in urban areas had broken down. Mineworkers were kept on low wages because, it was argued, their main income came from land and cattle held in the reserves, where their families continued to subsist. In reality, as the 1944 Lansdown Commission acknowledged, the reserves

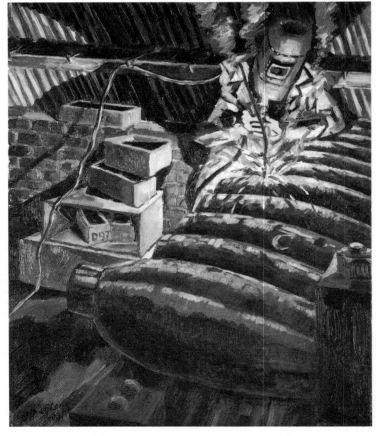

could no longer supplement migrant workers' wages as most migrants were landless.

African workers became increasingly militant during and after the war. War Measure 145 had been introduced to prohibit strikes by Africans, following a wave of unrest in 1942. Bus boycotts in Pretoria and on the Witwatersrand drew attention to the high cost of travel and as a result the Public Utility Transport Corporation (PUTCO) was set up to provide a subsidised bus service for African workers. The 1946 mineworkers' strike immobilised ten gold mines and cut production in many more. This strike involved 73,000 mineworkers who were protesting against low wages, poor food and dangerous working conditions. The effect of this increasing militancy was to further radicalise the membership of the African National Congress. The Youth League of the ANC took a more extreme position than its elders.

It is ironic that the Smuts Government was the most liberal South Africa had known. Yet in 1947 when Smuts offered the

Above: Dr D F Malan and his family at Groote Schuur, the Prime Minister's residence and once the property of Cecil Rhodes.

Above right: A contemporary cartoon captures the public irritation at the complacency and lethargy of the ruling United Party. It was to prove fatal in the 1948 General Election.

Left: Baton-wielding police keep a wary eye on demonstrators protesting outside the House of Representatives against the Group Areas Bill and anti-communist legislation.

Native Representative Council enlarged membership, he still could not countenance the idea of citizenship for blacks. Similarly the Government curtailed land rights for Indians both in Natal and the Transvaal, and when it held out the carrot of parliamentary representation the Government was rebuffed by the Indian leaders.

Clearly the Smuts Government, although it had a comfortable majority in Parliament, had no mandate for a more liberal policy towards blacks. The United Party had apparently won a clear mandate in the 1943 election, but today historians see in the result clear forebodings of the Party's defeat five years later. In fact the Nationalists had consolidated their position as the main opposition party, with 43 seats. The Labour Party was eliminated as the workers' party, and this meant that there was a swing in white working-class support to the Nationalists.

The 1948 election was fought by the Nationalists on their policy of apartheid or separate development. Although ill-defined before the election, apartheid nevertheless appealed to a broad spectrum of opinion, mostly farmers and semi-skilled

workers who felt threatened by the 'liberal' measures implemented during the war.

To broaden the appeal Dr Malan soft-pedalled the hard republican line, promising that South Africa would remain a member of the Commonwealth and professing support for the principle of equal language-rights for English-speakers. While Malan's stance may not have won many English-speakers' votes it undoubtedly placated moderate Afrikaners, thereby ensuring the National Party an electoral pact with the Afrikaner Party. In marked contrast the United Party was beset with a number of social and economic problems relating to the demands of a country and population adjusting to the post-war world.

The National Party won 70 seats, and the Afrikaner Party nine, against the United Party's 65 and the Labour Party's six seats. The victory was gained with the support of about 40 per cent of the electorate, and it seemed to the United Party that without too much effort it could reverse the verdict at the next election. The defeat of the United Party was, however, to prove irreversible.

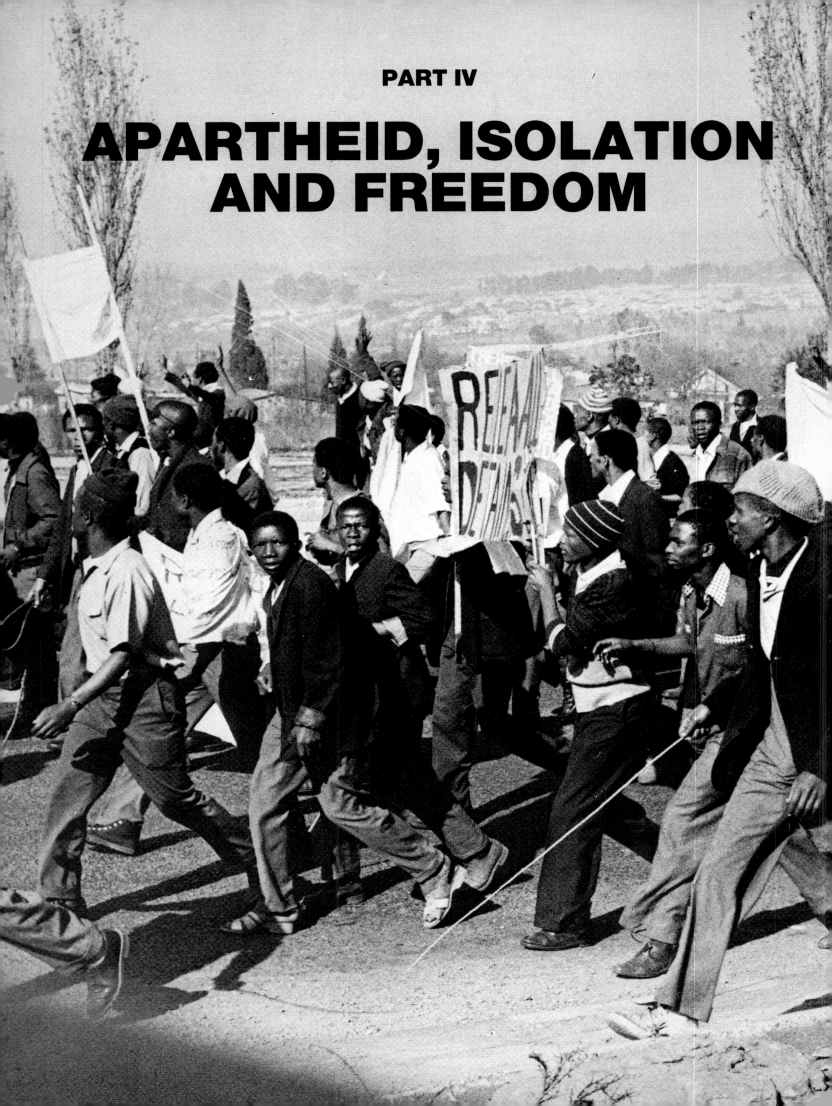

PART IV
APARTHEID, ISOLATION AND FREEDOM

THE NEW ASCENDANCY

The 1948 election was hailed by many Afrikaners as much more than a mere political victory. It was the crowning achievement of half a century of struggle and deprivation.

Dr Malan wasted no time in defining his policy of apartheid and in introducing legislation to give it a legal framework. A first step was to create machinery for preventing the intermingling of races in white areas. 'Mixed' marriages between whites and blacks were prohibited in 1949, and a year later the Immorality Act of 1927 was amended to ban 'immoral' acts between whites and blacks. Under the 1950 Population Registration Act every individual was classified according to race, with a Race Classification Board set up to adjudicate on borderline cases. The object seems to have been to prevent Coloureds from registering as whites, but instead it succeeded in causing great misery to people who had previously 'passed for white'.

To implement the grand design of physical separation of the races the Group Areas Act was passed in 1950. As a means of removing black communities living in 'white' areas to their own separate areas it proved particularly effective. Possibly the best known of the laws of this period was the Separate Amenities Act of 1953 which regulated public amenities; overseas critics of apartheid were appalled by *Blankes Alleen* (Whites Only) notices on park benches, and by the use of

Above: Separate facilities in public buildings such as post offices were soon part of the scene as the Malan Government translated the informal colour bar into legislation.

Left: White children were nearly all brought up from infancy by black servants, but soon discovered that the outside world was strictly segregated.

Right: Failure to produce a valid pass made urban blacks liable to arrest. The pass laws put every law-abiding black at risk, but did little to cut crime as forged documents were widely available.

Previous pages: In August 1976 serious unrest broke out in Soweto, south west of Johannesburg.

Above: The 1951 Cabinet included two future Prime Ministers, J G Strijdom (Min. of Lands and Irrigation) and H F Verwoerd (Min. of Native Affairs), and a future State President, C R Swart (Min. of Justice).

separate entrances for whites and blacks to public buildings such as post offices. But of all the legislation introduced to implement apartheid the so-called 'Pass Laws' of 1952 proved the most unpopular. These laws compelled blacks to carry identification documents at all times — an effective means of establishing precisely where black people lived and worked. One justification for this cumbersome procedure was that it would help in the prevention of crime, although many critics pointed out that no black professional criminal was ever apprehended because he lacked a valid pass.

One of the major milestones of apartheid was the removal of Coloured voters from the common voting roll. In 1951 Dr Dönges introduced the Separate Representation of Voters Bill, under which Coloured voters were to be transferred to a separate voting roll. The Opposition argued against the legislation, insisting that such a major constitutional amendment must be ratified by a two-thirds majority of a joint sitting of the House of Assembly and the Senate. As the Government did not possess such a majority it was tempted to ignore the objections, declaring that Parliament was sovereign and could not allow itself to be bound by what it called the 'dead hand of the past'.

This unusual interpretation of the entrenched clauses of the Constitution did not silence opposition. Although an application by two Coloured voters to have the legislation set aside was defeated in the Cape Division of the Supreme Court, the Appeal Court found against the Government in March 1952. The Malan Government was in a dilemma: public opinion would not have accepted the dismissal of the Appeal Court judges, but the Government did not have the requisite two-thirds majority.

The solution, when the two-thirds majority still eluded the Government after another general election, was to appoint six new Appeal Court judges and 45 extra senators. These shoddy manoeuvres were fiercely denounced by the Opposition and

the English-language press, but to no avail. Contemporary feeling among the English-speaking population was one of deep unease, even guilt. Inevitably the Coloured community was even more alienated from the Afrikaners. Apart from the injustice, it was imprudent for the whites to discount the support of a group of people whose background should have made them natural allies.

The principal objectives of the Act, which finally reached the statute book in 1956, were to remove the Cape Province Coloureds from the common voters' roll, and to place them on a separate roll. The Cape would be divided into four Coloured electoral divisions, each of which would elect a white representative to the House of Assembly. Coloureds would also be able to elect three white representatives to the Cape Provincial Council. As a further sop a nationwide Council for Coloured Affairs would be set up.

The National Party showed no sign of weakening. When D F Malan retired from politics in 1954 his successor was the ardent republican J G Strijdom. The 'Lion of the North' represented the hard-line associated with the Transvaal — white hegemony at any cost. This development was as much as anything a gesture of defiance to mounting criticism of South Africa's colour policy abroad. Under his leadership support for the National Party increased steadily, and in the 1958 election for the first time the National Party overtook the United Party, winning 55 per cent of the votes.

Strijdom did not live to enjoy the fruits of victory. He died in August 1958 and was succeeded by Dr H F Verwoerd.

Above: Johannes Strijdom succeeded Malan as Prime Minister in 1954. The 'Lion of the North' increased the Nad volunteers guarding grazing draught oxen.

Right: The Women's Defence of the Constitution League march through Johannesburg wearing black sashes in mourning for the damage done to the Constitution by the Senate Act.

Left: Indian women attending a political rally in 1948. As successful entrepreneurs the Indian community was hard-hit by apartheid legislation, but failed to find common ground with the blacks.

Above left: The Torch Commando was a short-lived anti-government movement. Made up largely of ex-servicemen, it failed to find sufficient political support among Afrikaners.

SEPARATE DEVELOPMENT BECOMES A REALITY

Although the 1948 election manifesto of the National Party outlined the principle that black people should, as far as possible, be settled in their 'respective' territories, the concept did not take form until Dr H F Verwoerd became Minister of Native Affairs in 1950. The Tomlinson Commission presented a detailed report in 1954, recommending fully separated development for the black population.

A key element of the proposals was an urgent programme of investment to develop the black areas, using both public and private capital to stimulate industry. The Tomlinson Report put a figure of R200 million for investment, spread over a period of ten years. While several of the recommendations were accepted, the scale of investment was derisory: R7 million for the first year, and nothing thereafter. Nor was private enterprise to make up the deficit; the Government feared that whites would exploit blacks and try to take control of their businesses. However, as a compromise, 'border industries' were permitted close to the borders of black areas.

Above: The new National Party cabinet after the 1958 election. Dr Verwoerd is in the front row, third from left.

Left: Professor F R Tomlinson chaired a commission whose report became the basis of separate development.

Verwoerd's ideas were much more radical than many whites realised. Unlike many of his fellow Afrikaners he accepted as logical and inevitable the creation of self-governing black countries within the borders of South Africa — areas that became known as 'Bantustans'. Verwoerd was committed to the policy, and in 1959 he introduced his Promotion of Bantu Self-Government Act. Black people were to be divided into eight ethnic units, each administered by a Commissioner-General. These administrators were to be the link between the Government in Pretoria and their ethnic units and would be responsible for economic development.

In addition to the undemocratic and unjust nature of the plan, a practical flaw in the Tomlinson Report was a serious underestimate of the growth-rate of the African population.

Figures compiled from the 1970 Census showed that there would be 37 million blacks by the end of the century, rather than the figure of 21 million assumed by Tomlinson. The revelation caused Verwoerd's successor, B J Vorster, to accelerate the process of moving 'surplus' blacks out of white areas.

In 1967 magistrates were given four categories of Africans who qualified for removal: the elderly, unfit and dependant, who did not qualify to live in towns; redundant labourers on white-owned farms; inhabitants of 'black spots' in white areas; and professional people whose skills were needed in the homelands. These forced evictions were to be linked to a new concept of citizenship, conferred by each independent homeland on its inhabitants. Even blacks living outside the homeland would qualify for citizenship if they spoke its language at

Right: Segregated hostels for single black workers in Alexandra Township, to the north of Johannesburg. The barbaric practice of separating married women and men from their families created immense social problems.

Left: Evicted blacks look on as their houses are demolished to conform with the provisions of the Group Areas Act. Resettlement has caused great distress.

Above: Alan Paton, author of *Cry the Beloved Country*, addresses a mixed-race meeting in Johannesburg to protest against forced clearances.

Right: One of the shanty towns outside Cape Town. Many blacks are forced to live in these squalid conditions.

home. Any African who lost South African citizenship in this way would be allowed back into the Republic only if work was available, and then on annually renewable contracts. The effect of this legislation was to force Africans working in South Africa to break their stay, thus effectively preventing them from acquiring 'Section 10' rights under the Urban Areas Act. These rights would have been awarded to someone living continuously in an urban area for 15 years or working continuously for one employer for ten years.

As if this minefield of regulations was not enough the 1968 Physical Planning Act tried to stimulate 'border industries' through tax concessions and offers of cheap labour. The scheme was not a success, generating fewer than 8000 jobs per year between 1960 and 1972 (the Tomlinson Report had called for 50,000 jobs per year). Distress was widespread, for the removals were on a huge scale; some resettlement areas would contain up to 200,000 people living in dire poverty.

Severe drought increased the hardships of people resettled on poor farming land, and a catastrophic fall in the gold price from $850 an ounce in 1980 to $300 two years later cut the nation's resources. In any case, the Government failed to anticipate the problems caused by their 'ethnic cleansing' policy, and did not provide sufficient money to bring about the rapid improvements that were needed.

SOUTH AFRICA BECOMES A REPUBLIC

It was a supreme irony that in 1960, at the beginning of the fiftieth anniversary of the Union, Dr Verwoerd chose to announce a referendum on a change from dominion status to a republic. His argument throughout was that the peculiar status of the Union fostered divisions between English- and Afrikaans-speakers. This line of reasoning appealed to a number of otherwise staunch opponents of the Government, who were reinforced by an unrealistic assumption that South Africa might emulate India and somehow remain in the Commonwealth with ties to the Crown.

In fact Verwoerd and the National Party had no serious intention of remaining in the Commonwealth, which was now dominated largely by newly independent African states that showed unremitting hostility to South Africa. Indeed, Britain was divesting herself of colonial responsibilities as fast as possible. The British Prime Minister Harold Macmillan made his famous 'Wind of Change' speech in Parliament in February 1960, only a month after the announcement of the referen-

Above: Dr Verwoerd with the British Prime Minister Harold Macmillan during his February 1960 visit. The 'Wind of Change' speech was a sharp reminder to English-speakers that the old ways would soon have to change forever.

Left: A pro-apartheid poster prominently displayed in South Africa in the late 1950s.

Above: David Pratt, who failed in his bid to assassinate Dr Verwoerd in 1960. His motive was personal, and he later committed suicide in a mental clinic.

Left: Verwoerd was shot at the Rand Easter Show on 9 April 1960, but he survived two small-calibre bullets in the head at close range.

dum. He warned that African nationalism was a powerful force which Britain could not ignore in her international relations. The message to white South Africans was clear; Britain could no longer be looked to as a guarantor of their way of life or even as a champion in the councils of the Commonwealth. Verwoerd's reply was terse but summed up the dilemma of the Afrikaner nation. He reminded Macmillan that there must be justice for the white man as well as the black. Afrikaners had nowhere else to go; for them, South Africa was their motherland.

Against a background of increasing violence the plans for the referendum went ahead. Scarcely a week after Sharpeville, a serious incident when police killed many demonstrators (see next chapter), Verwoerd was seriously wounded by two shots fired by a rich English-speaking farmer, David Pratt. Miraculously two bullets in the head failed to kill the Prime Minister, who resumed official duties a few weeks later. What was even more surprising was the calm, almost indifference,

with which the assassination attempt was greeted by the English-speaking population, most of whom regarded it as no more than could be expected, given the extreme dislike many felt for Verwoerd and his republican plans.

The referendum confirmed this deep split; over 90 per cent of the whites cast their votes (only whites, including those in South West Africa, were eligible), yet the margin was only 74,580 for the republic. Johannesburg, for example, voted heavily against, and Natal as a whole voted against – the only province to do so; the Orange Free State and the Transvaal both voted massively in favour. What was equally clear was that Verwoerd and his political plans had persuaded many waverers among the English-speaking community to come off the fence.

Events moved swiftly. In January 1961 legislation was tabled and on 31 May the Republic of South Africa became a reality. The Commonwealth Conference held in London in March resulted in anti-South African delegates making conditions that Dr Verwoerd would not accept, and as a result South Africa's membership of the Commonwealth terminated with the formal creation of the Republic. The former Justice Minister C R Swart was sworn in as the first State President of the new Republic of South Africa.

The economic consequences of withdrawal from the Commonwealth were not serious. Macmillan had given an assurance that bilateral trade agreements in force since the Ottawa Conference in 1932 would be honoured. Britain was not alone in needing South Africa's gold and raw materials. As a sop to English-speakers' feelings Verwoerd appointed two English-speaking members to his first republican Cabinet, but the blacks were understandably dismayed at the outcome. To Afrikaners on the far right of the party it might seem that the verdict of the Anglo-Boer War had been reversed (as some stated publicly) but blacks knew that they now had no hope of fundamental reform from above.

One of the two white tribes had satisfied its national aspirations, the second was now a reluctant partner in this unhappy alliance, and the other tribes had no choice but to look elsewhere for sympathy.

Left: C R Swart was the last Governor-General and the first State President of the new Republic.

Below: Government supporters in Pretoria celebrate the declaration of the Republic on 31 May 1961. In Cape Town, Durban, Johannesburg and Pietermaritzburg enthusiasm was more muted.

THE ROAD TO ISOLATION

Left: The scene at Sharpeville as demonstrators fled from police gunfire.

Below: The judicial enquiry into the Sharpeville incident found no evidence of a deliberate policy to shoot without warning. Yet the tragedy has gone down in history as a massacre.

Bottom: South Africa's talks with Chief Leabua Jonathan of Lesotho in 1966 were compromised when Verwoerd was assassinated a few days later.

The 'Wind of Change' was no empty political rhetoric. What Macmillan had tried to warn of in 1960 was the reality of the world in the second half of the century. It was easy to dismiss the United Nations as a talking-shop but when in 1960 police opened fire on demonstrators in the African 'townships' of Sharpeville and Langa (the reason has never been disclosed), criticism was heard from around the world. The shootings revealed the contempt of the new republic for the civil and democratic rights of its black population and not even South Africa's friends could ignore the deaths of 70 people.

An unexpected result of the international campaign against South Africa was to force Pretoria to reassess its attitude to its neighbours. Initially this took the form of closer ties with Portugal, but the international community regarded Portuguese rule in Mozambique as equally obnoxious. Under Dr Verwoerd there was little or no attempt to establish links with black African states. An approach by Nigeria in 1962 and another in 1964 by Zambia were both rebuffed. However when Britain granted independence to her three protectorates Lesotho (Basutoland), Botswana (Bechuanaland) and Swaziland in the mid-1960s, South Africa responded by immediately recognising them as sovereign states, and pledged to maintain good relations.

In 1966 Chief Leabua Jonathan, Chief Minister of Lesotho, was invited to Pretoria for talks, but the assassination of Dr Verwoerd a few days later aborted any understanding which had been under negotiation. Diplomatic relations were not established with Lesotho, Botswana or Swaziland, but the following year Malawi became the first black state to establish diplomatic ties with South Africa.

By 1966 there were 40 new black states in Africa, and their pressure through the Organisation of African Unity could no longer be ignored. In practice South Africa had become overdependent on the support of the United States, France and Britain at the Security Council of the UN, and it was clear that better relations were now an urgent need. South Africa's

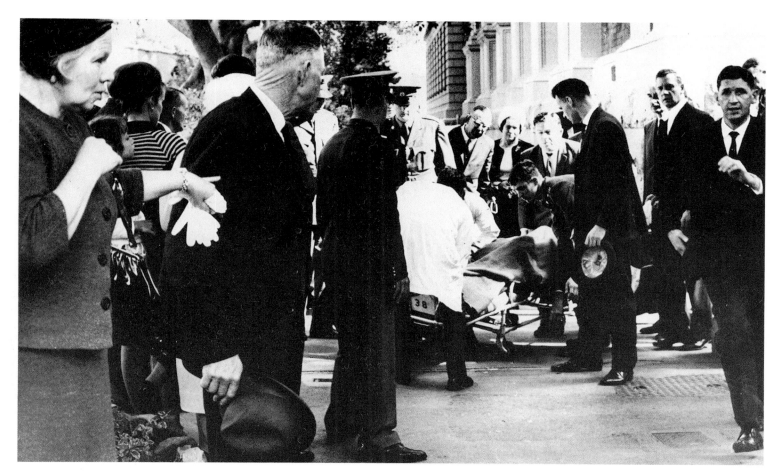

Above: The second attempt to assassinate Dr Verwoerd succeeded in 1966. A white government employee stabbed him in the House of Assembly in Cape Town.

Right: The ex-OB general B J Vorster succeeded Verwoerd in 1966. As Minister of Justice he had already introduced new repressive security laws, a trend which was to continue.

rulers also wished to make South Africa the dominant force in a southern African economic area, hoping to create a buffer zone of friendly capitalist states. The country's industries would benefit from new outlets for its manufacturers, and from cheap migrant labour, while evidence of more normal and stable relations with African states would encourage foreign investment.

The *coup d'état* in Portugal in 1974 and the establishment of a Marxist regime in Maputo (as Lourenço Marques was re-named) raised the spectre of a long frontier open to attack. Coupled with the failure of Rhodesian whites to defeat a nationalist guerrilla campaign, the Portuguese withdrawal meant that the buffer-strip on the country's northern and eastern flank no longer existed.

The challenge was met with vigour. Prime Minister Vorster announced a new policy of détente, with an emphasis on stability and co-operation. In September 1974 he visited the Ivory Coast for talks with President Houphouet-Boigny and on his way back stopped briefly in Gabon, Botswana and Rhodesia. Even the Marxist President Samora Michel of Mozambique was wooed, but like other black leaders he had no wish to collaborate with the apartheid government in Pretoria. Only a handful of leaders were prepared to do so; others co-operated in secret and the rest remained hostile.

Vorster's policy of détente was unsuccessful. The intervention in the Angolan civil war in 1975 was made at the request

Right: To support new harsh laws police strength was reinforced. These Johannesburg traffic police are equipped as an auxiliary riot squad, with shields, batons and riot shotguns.

Below: B J Vorster and President Kaunda of Zambia were briefly united in their efforts to put pressure on Ian Smith and the rebels to bring the Rhodesian guerrilla war to an end.

of Zambia, Zaire and the USA, but the majority of African states secured a UN Security Council resolution condemning the intervention. Tough police action in suppressing the Soweto unrest in 1976 further inflamed overseas opinion, and in November 1977 the UN General Assembly voted for a mandatory arms embargo.

The new president P W Botha and his Foreign Minister 'Pik' Botha pursued a more pragmatic policy, continuing low-key negotiations with neighbouring states but making it clear on numerous occasions that these states should not become sanctuaries for terrorists and guerrillas. It soon became clear, however, that South Africa was deliberately destabilising regimes by funding and supporting dissident movements such as RENAMO in Mozambique and UNITA in Angola.

For South Africa's neighbours being a front-line state was ruinously expensive. Their dilemma was that while they were economically dependent on South Africa, peace would have implied acceptance of the brutal suppression of their fellow black Africans. Botswana, Lesotho and Swaziland each obtain 90 per cent or more of their imports through South Africa, and the money earned by migrant workers is vital to the economies of Mozambique, Malawi, Zimbabwe and the homelands. The neighbouring states also rely heavily on South Africa's advanced rail and road network.

South Africa's unwillingness to allow its neighbours to determine their own affairs has caused untold misery in Angola and Mozambique in particular. One of South Africa's reasons for doing this was the desire to destroy ANC military bases in these countries. But by forcing the ANC underground, turning what was originally a peaceful protest movement into an exiled terrorist organisation, South Africa could only blame itself for creating this external threat.

Above: Police manhandle a black demonstrator as the Soweto riots continue to gather momentum.

Right: Casspir armoured personnel carriers move into Soweto to put down demonstrations.

THE RISE OF BLACK NATIONALISM

Left: Indian and Coloured leaders were early victims of the anti-Communist legislation. Left to right: Dr Y Dadoo, J Phillips, J B Marks, Nana Sita and Dr Moroka.

Right: Burning the hated passbooks led to the mass demonstrations at Langa and Sharpeville in 1960. The police powers of summary arrest under the Pass Laws was subsequently curtailed.

Below: Alan Paton's novel *Cry the Beloved Country* was filmed by the British director Zoltan Korda (left). It was widely shown in South Africa but had no influence in Government circles.

After the National Party's victory in 1948 it was the African National Congress that took the lead in campaigning for black political power. Its Youth League planned a militant programme of strikes, public disobedience and boycotts. The main objectives of the ANC were stated to be freedom from white domination and the achievement of representation in all official institutions.

The first direct action took place in 1950 when, tragically, 18 strikers were killed on the Witwatersrand. In that year the Communist Party was proscribed under the Suppression of Communism Act. In 1951 the ANC, the Indian Congress and the Franchise Action Council, under the umbrella of the Joint Planning Council, started a campaign of resistance to the new discriminatory legislation. During the following months a campaign against the pass laws gathered momentum, with offenders refusing to pay fines.

The Government clamped down on all resistance movements, and imprisoned several black, Coloured and Asian leaders. The Joint Planning Council's campaign failed to get any apartheid legislation repealed or even modified, but it attracted attention abroad. It also led to the formation of two new political parties, Alan Paton's multi-racial Liberals and the radical pro-Communist Congress of Democrats. Membership of the ANC expanded as well.

The resistance campaigns were not helped by the deep internal rifts that existed among the various participants. The

Congress of the People, another broad alliance, produced a Freedom Charter, a moderate affirmation of a form of social democracy, but this document alienated the radical black nationalists who rejected its appeal for racial co-operation within a white-ruled state. In 1958-59 this rift came to a head with the formation of the breakaway Pan Africanist Congress (PAC) under the leadership of Robert Sobukwe. He was to state bluntly, 'We claim Africa for the Africans, the ANC claims

South Africa for All'. Unlike the ANC, then led by Nelson Mandela and Albert Luthuli, the PAC disliked the idea of collaborating with Asians and Coloureds.

After the brutality of Sharpeville the Government declared a state of emergency, called out the Active Citizen Force and banned public meetings. Although the pass laws were relaxed temporarily to rob the pass-burning campaign of its impact, over 11,000 people were detained. The ANC and PAC were proscribed under new legislation, the Unlawful Organisations Act, and both organisations were driven underground. Nelson Mandela, known for his ability to stay at large as the 'Black Pimpernel', was finally arrested in 1962. Two years later police discovered evidence that the military wing of the ANC, *Umkhonto We Sizwe* (Spear of the Nation), was planning a campaign of sabotage under Mandela's direction. In the 'Rivonia Trial' documents in Mandela's handwriting were produced and the leader of the ANC was sentenced to life imprisonment on Robben Island.

Whereas Mandela's sabotage campaign was aimed at petrol dumps, railways, power supplies and government buildings, the parallel *Poqo* organisation set up by PAC extremists pursued a policy of undisguised terrorism. It achieved limited success but like the ANC its efforts were severely circumscribed by constant police counter-action.

A new threat developed in Namibia (still officially South West Africa), with a campaign of sabotage and terrorism

Above: Robert Sobukwe, an outstanding black intellectual, launched the breakaway Pan Africanist Congress in 1958. He was sentenced to three years' imprisonment on Robben Island, then banned for another three years. He spent the remaining 14 years of his life under house arrest.

Right: Weapon training for young ANC guerrillas, probably in Zambia or Mozambique.

Left and far left: Nelson Mandela was a founder member of the ANC Youth League in 1944, becoming its president in 1950. After 17 months in hiding he was arrested in 1962, and later received a life sentence for planning the ANC sabotage campaign. He was finally released in 1990 and became the first black president of South Africa after the elections in 1994.

Right: A massive police presence guarded the Pretoria Supreme Court during the trial of Nelson Mandela in 1964.

Top and above: Steve Biko died in Pretoria in September 1977 but his fatal injuries were inflicted in Port Elizabeth, many hundreds of miles away.

Right: Oliver Tambo graduated in Law with Nelson Mandela at the University of the Witwatersrand. For many years he led the ANC from exile.

initiated by the South West African People's Organisation (SWAPO). Like the ANC and PAC they used bases in Angola and Zambia, provoking retaliatory raids.

With most of the political leaders in prison or in exile it seemed that the Government had broken the back of resistance, but in mid-1976 large-scale violence erupted in Soweto, the sprawling urban housing development for blacks south-west of Johannesburg. Ostensibly the rioters were protesting at the compulsory use of Afrikaans in schools but there were so many grievances that any one could suffice. In the ensuing unrest the police killed 700 blacks, many of them juveniles armed only with stones.

Equally disturbing to the black population was the death of Steve Biko in police custody. Biko had done much to create the Black Consciousness movement which was derived from American blacks' experience in the Civil Rights movement. His charisma helped to stimulate a new awareness and sense of pride among urban blacks that did much to counter the demoralisation brought about by poverty and the injustices of apartheid. The refusal of the Minister of Justice and the police to produce any satisfactory explanation for Biko's death caused many Government supporters to express doubts about the society they had created. In fact he was only one of 50 who had died in police detention.

WAR BEYOND THE BORDERS

The withdrawal of the Portuguese from Angola in 1975 left the Marxist MPLA, who had been fighting a war of liberation since 1961, in control of the capital, Luanda, and much of northern Angola. There were, however, also two non-Marxist liberation movements, FNLA and UNITA, and fighting broke out between the Marxist and non-Marxist factions. At first the UNITA-FNLA forces did well, as the South African Defence Force had invaded Angola to support them. They advanced almost to the suburbs of Luanda before Cuban reinforcements and the MPLA, re-equipped with Russian weaponry, were able to push back the rebels. South African troops had been secretly ordered into Angola in July supposedly to cover the withdrawal of political refugees and to guard the incomplete Calueque Dam. However, when the MPLA leadership gave an undertaking to safeguard the construction workers, these defensive positions were abandoned and South African troops advanced towards Luanda.

Left: The Defence Minister, Lt-General Magnus Malan, made the South African Defence Force the most formidable military force in Africa. During the 1970s and 80s the Army's political influence increased at the expense of the Police.

Below: The arming and reinforcing of the Marxist People's Liberation Army by Cuba and the Soviet Union followed South African intervention in Angola after the defeat of the Portuguese.

In February 1976 the MPLA was internationally recognised as the legitimate Government of Angola, but this did not bring the war to an end, for the UNITA forces under Jonas Savimbi, backed by South Africa, chose to fight on. The Cubans did not leave Angola either, and South Africa became more involved in the war, supporting UNITA at first covertly and later waging an independent campaign with her own troops. The failure of the US Government to support South Africa became a bone of contention between Pretoria and Washington, and it was not until the Reagan Administration replaced President Carter's Democrats that the policy changed.

In 1985 South African troops won a decisive victory at Mavinga, using C-130 Hercules transports to fly in weapons, ammunition and supplies to UNITA. By August that year South African support was out in the open; the Defence Minister General Magnus Malan stated that his forces would intervene 'militarily and without limit' to save UNITA and Savimbi.

The scope of the conflict began to widen. From March 1986 American war material began to reach UNITA, and in August the 32nd 'Buffalo' Battalion, backed by artillery, attacked Cuito Cuanavale. Furthermore, a seaborne force attacked three Soviet ships at Namibe, sinking one of them.

However, in 1987 the war bogged down; the MPLA Government could not be beaten because of its massive Soviet and Cuban support, but neither could Savimbi be beaten while South Africa and the United States supported him.

In 1988, after a major South African military defeat, talks began to end the war. South African spokesmen offered a

Right: South African troops preparing to withdraw from Angola.

Above: Jonas Savimbi, head of the UNITA anti-Marxist guerrillas in Angola, and South Africa's ally.

Left: UNITA's troops did well with South African support but the war bogged down in 1987. The South Africans began talks with the MPLA and the Cubans in 1988, leading to an agreement for both sides to withdraw in 1989.

Right: UNITA's guerrillas were too strong to be beaten but not strong enough to defeat the Soviet-backed Cubans and MPLA.

guaranteed departure of their forces from Angola provided it was matched by a similar withdrawal of the Cubans. The Cubans insisted upon Namibian independence and the implementation of UN Resolution 435.

These talks eventually led to a ceasefire on 31 May 1991 after 16 years of civil war, and then elections in September 1992. President José Eduardo dos Santos and the MPLA won the elections, but after protracted peace talks UNITA refused to accept the results and decided to continue the civil war, despite recognition of the dos Santos government by the US in May 1993. In the late summer of 1994 the fighting was still raging.

In a similar attempt to destabilize a neighbouring socialist country, South Africa gave support to the rebel RENAMO movement in Mozambique in the 1980s. Largely created by Rhodesian security forces in 1978 to fight the Frelimo government and Zimbabwean nationalists, RENAMO moved their headquarters to South Africa after Zimbabwean independence, and continued their brutal campaign of terror with large-scale South African assistance.

In 1984 President Machel concluded a peace treaty, the Nkomati Accord. It was supposed to secure an end to support for RENAMO in return for an end to support for ANC guerrillas, but relations with South Africa remained difficult. By repatriating an estimated 60,000 migrant workers, South Africa inflicted a devastating blow on the Mozambique economy — migrant workers' remittances accounted for a third of the country's foreign earnings.

South Africa was blamed for the air crash that killed Presi-

Above: Despite accusations of South African involvement in President Machel's death, the likely cause was a pilot error.

dent Machel in 1986, but impartial investigators later established that the most likely cause was an error by the Russian pilot. Nevertheless, in 1985 the Gorongosa documents revealed continuing South African involvement with RENAMO. In 1989, the United Nations estimated that the war had led to 494,000 children under five being killed, a million refugees, and perhaps another million deaths. Much of RENAMO's army was composed of kidnapped people, many of them children who had been forced to kill their relatives and other children. The US deputy assistant secretary of state, Roy Stacey, has called the war 'one of the most brutal holocausts against ordinary human beings since World War II', and a US state department report in 1988 held RENAMO responsible for 100,000 civilian deaths.

In 1990, a new multi-party constitution was approved and the Mozambique government and RENAMO began negotiations in Rome. In the ensuing Rome Agreement of 1992 President Joachim Chissano and the RENAMO leader Alfonso Dhaklama both agreed to demobilise in the run up to an election scheduled for October 1994. There is considerable pressure from the US and the UN for both parties to form a government of national unity after the elections in the hope that this ravaged country can finally find peace.

NAMIBIA

From 1966 to 1989 the South West Africa People's Organisation (SWAPO) waged a guerrilla war against South African security forces – the longest campaign in African history. The guerrillas operated during the rainy season, between December and April, using the dense undergrowth for cover, and taking advantage of the heavy seasonal downpours.

In 1971, the International Court of Justice ruled South Africa's occupation of Namibia illegal, but South Africa refused to withdraw and pressed on with its plans to introduce apartheid to Namibia with the creation of ten 'tribal homelands'. Naturally SWAPO regarded the Multi-Party Conference (MPC) politicians who participated in this plan as collaborators. SWAPO's claim that they are the sole representatives of the Namibian people, was supported by the MPLA in Luanda, who permitted PLAN guerrillas to operate from bases in southern Angola, but SWAPO's military effectiveness was weakened by internal dissent. Various factions, on several occasions, betrayed SWAPO and PLAN operations to the Government forces, and undercover agents repeatedly penetrated the organisation.

It would be wrong to infer that SWAPO was ineffectual, however. The cost of the counter-insurgency action was estimated at $550 million per annum, and some 3000 South African servicemen died from enemy action and disease.

Namibia has been a pressing issue for South Africa. In 1974 the Security Council adopted a resolution demanding that independence should be granted within six months, following negotiations with the front-line states. The following year, at the Turnhalle Conference in Windhoek, a constitution was drafted that was acceptable to the whites of Namibia but not to

Above: Daniel Tjongarero, Deputy Chairman of SWAPO, was detained after a bomb explosion in Windhoek in 1978.

Left: Demonstrators in Dar-es-Salaam celebrate the fifth anniversary of the founding of the Organisation of African Unity in 1963.

Above: SWAPO supporters at a rally outside Windhoek in 1986 mark the 20th anniversary of the war against South Africa.

Left: A mounted Ovambo soldier near the Angolan border, looking for PLAN guerrillas.

Right: Well-armed and trained black troops of the South West Africa Territory Force.

SWAPO or the UN. Deadlock seemed complete, with South Africa refusing to implement any UN resolutions until the Cubans had left Angola. The MPLA initially refused to admit that the presence of Cuban troops in Angola was anything but an internal matter.

In the summer of 1988, however, after a South African military defeat in Angola, South African and Cuban representatives met with MPLA and UNITA spokesmen in Brazzaville to discuss a ceasefire. South Africa expressed her willingness to link a withdrawal from Angola (to comply with UN Resolution 435) with a firm date for Namibian independence. The long-running Namibian problem will, hopefully, be solved by the December 1988 accord, which led to Namibia's first free elections in November 1989.

These elections resulted in a majority for SWAPO, but they did not have unanimous support throughout Nambia. In March 1990, the new president, Sam Nujoma, declared Namibia independent, and although there was still some unfinished business with South Africa over the Walvis Bay naval base, the more liberal South African government of the 1990s decided to pursue the matter by dialogue rather than destabilisation. The prospects for lasting peace in Namibia look good.

Left: Ovambo delegates to the Turnhalle Conference in 1975. Its draft constitution was rejected by the United Nations and SWAPO.

SOME MINOR REFORMS

Although Prime Minister Vorster was no apostle of reform his administration did try to get rid of 'petty apartheid' and put forward modest proposals to improve the constitutional position of the Coloureds. These were adopted after a white referendum accepted the points first raised by a commission headed by Dr Erika Theron, which urged reforms such as the removal of the ban on mixed white and Coloured audiences, and the inclusion of Coloureds in white sports teams.

The white ranks were still deeply divided, however, and the Government's supporters in particular. The *verligtes* (enlightened) were bitterly opposed by the *verkramptes* (narrow-minded) among the Nationalists. For the *verligtes* 'petty apartheid', the panoply of pass laws, separate amenities and so forth, could safely be abandoned without endangering the survival of the Afrikaner nation, whereas for the *verkramptes* apartheid was a creed to be defended in every detail. Led by Dr Albert Hertzog (son of General Hertzog) the *Herstigte* (Refounded) National Party broke away from what they regarded

Left: Dr Eschel Roodie, a leading figure in the 'Muldergate' scandal.

Below left: The resignation of B J Vorster in 1978 cleared the way for P W Botha, the Defence Minister, to become Prime Minister. Unlike Vorster his power-base was the Army.

Below: 'Connie' Mulder was forced to resign as Minister of Information and his ministry was closed down. He retaliated with claims that Vorster and others were fully implicated in the scandal to appropriate public funds.

as the deviations and weaknesses of Verwoerd's successors.

The 'Muldergate' scandal of 1978 discredited the Vorster Government by its revelations of corruption and extra-Parliamentary action. Vorster resigned in time to avoid full implication and was succeeded by P W Botha, leader of the Cape Nationalists and Minister of Defence. His links with the SADF gave him a power-base which did not rely on the support of the police. There had been rumours at the time of the Soweto riots of friction between the police and the military; the latter resented having to 'clean up' after heavy-handed policing had, as they saw it, provoked the violent and prolonged disturbances in the township.

Above: Dr Andries Treurnicht, former Transvaal National Party leader, became a focus for right-wing fears about P W Botha's 'liberal' tendencies.

Left: Eugene Terre'Blanche's followers revive memories of Nazi Germany and the *Ossewabrandwag*.

Below: Students protest at Treurnicht's Bantu education policy.

Left: Archbishop Desmond Tutu, head of the Anglican Church in South Africa, is also General Secretary of the South African Council of Churches.

Right: President Botha visits Soweto in an effort to reassure white and black communities about reform.

Below right: The Urban Bantu Council sat once a week. It was a consultative body without legislative powers but some saw it as a first timid step along the road to self-government.

Below: A mixed race school in Woodstock, Cape Town.

P W Botha's first task was to tackle economic stagnation. Strict ideology had led the previous administration to neglect black urban settlements in order to stimulate economic activity in the homelands, but the homelands had been starved of capital as well. Contacts with the business community were fostered, efforts were made to open some jobs to blacks, and blacks were allowed collective bargaining rights. But this was really only tinkering with the edges of apartheid.

In 1982 even this slow pace of reform was threatened by a renewed outbreak of extreme political discord on the National Party's right wing. Dr Andries Treurnicht, leader of the Transvaal Nationalists, was determined to prevent Botha from implementing 'healthy power-sharing' between whites and blacks. By any but South African standards this was a very limited reform, for there was no intention of allowing power to slip from white hands, but it was sufficient to make Treurnicht form a new Conservative Party. The new party won key by-elections in the districts of Waterberg and Zoutpansberg, but even more worrying was the emergence of paramilitary movements reminiscent of the *Ossewabrandwag*, with similar symptoms of neo-Nazism.

In 1983, after a stiff fight with the Right and his own progressives, the Prime Minister won support for a new constitution (one that still excluded blacks from wider political life), with a two-thirds majority in the referendum. It provided for an executive State President (P W Botha was elected unanimously by the Electoral College) ruling over three legislative chambers. The House of Assembly was for white voters, the House of Representatives for Coloureds and the House of Delegates for Indians. To ensure white domination the House of Assembly was larger than the other two Houses together.

All members of the Cabinet were to be chosen by the President, and membership was not confined to MPs. The President's Council remained, most of its members being chosen by

the three chambers on a proportional basis, and a minority chosen partly by the President and partly by nomination.

The first test of the new constitution was the election of the Coloured and Indian representatives, which took place in the spring of 1984. The Rev. Allan Hendrickse's Labour Party was returned with a large majority, while Amichand Rajbansi's National People's Party won with a small majority – both polls had very low turnouts, however. P W Botha appointed the two leaders as Ministers without portfolio in South Africa's first multi-racial Cabinet, but he did not relinquish real power.

VIOLENCE, SANCTIONS AND STALEMATE

P W Botha's attempts to court the Coloured and Indian sections of the South African population with the new tricameral constitution were a failure. Less than 20 per cent of those eligible to vote actually did so, and by excluding blacks from the election this minor step in the right direction only served to highlight their powerless position. The House of Representatives and the House of Delegates were essentially talking shops with no real power, and the government's argument that blacks were already adequately represented through the homelands system convinced few. The fundamental structure of power remained unchanged.

Needless to say, the ANC and much of the black community were dismayed by the inadequacy of the reform. As is often the case in potentially revolutionary situations, tentative attempts at reform by authoritarian governments tend to exacerbate their problems rather than solve them, and the recently formed United Democratic Front (UDF) began to promote a 'culture of resistance' in the townships in response to the new constitution. The first mass political party since 1960, the UDF supported the Freedom Charter drawn up by the ANC in 1955, demanded an end to the apartheid system, and encompassed a broad range of civic, trade union, and church organisations which might have been represented by the ANC were it not banned. They were joined in their opposition to the new constitution by the more radical National Forum and the ANC itself, who called for its supporters to 'render South Africa ungovernable'.

From October 1984 serious unrest started to spread across the country from the townships in the Vaal triangle. This resistance began as a response to increases in rents, but peaceful rent boycotts and school protests were soon accompanied by attacks on government buildings and the homes of policemen. Perhaps most disturbing was the brutal assassination of local black councillors (who were often seen as collaborators) by the barbaric practice of 'necklacing', which involved placing a burning tyre around the victim's neck. The township revolt spread inexorably from Transvaal to the Orange Free State, the Cape and finally Natal.

The response of the security forces was severe. On the 25th anniversary of Sharpeville, in March 1985, a funeral procession in Uitenhage was fired upon by the police. Twenty people were killed. Angry township youths clashed with the police in the weeks that followed, and by July 1985 a State of Emergency was declared as parts of South Africa descended into virtual civil war. The government seemed unable to offer any solutions other than repression. By the time this State of Emergency had ended in March 1986, over 750 people had been killed and thousands had been imprisoned. The enduring legacy of the unrest was a culture of violence that became entrenched among township youths and increasing tension between elements of the black community, particularly between members of the Xhosa and Zulu tribes. There was, of course, also a deep distrust and hatred of the security forces. There were no tangible political victories for any faction.

Left: Hundreds of youths battle with heavily armed police in Crossroads squatter camp in February 1985. This was a common scene during the late 1980s.

Above: Black mourners carry the coffins of their comrades shot by the police in Uitenhage. Twenty were killed in one incident on 21 March 1985.

made it clear that foreign pressure would not make him yield to demands for meaningful reform and dismissed the idea of a majority-rule government.

The government had not only lost control in the townships, it had now lost the confidence of its own business community and the few remaining sympathetic ears abroad. Botha's stance finally brought the full-scale international sanctions that had threatened for so long. The US Congress forced Reagan to introduce trade sanctions, foreign companies and banks withdrew their investments, loans were called in, and credit was refused. As a result, the Rand plummeted, and the government was forced to suspend trading on the Johannesburg Stock Exchange.

The loss of business confidence led to extraordinary meetings in Lusaka between the ANC and representatives of South Africa's major industrial and commercial interests. The knowledge that the giant Anglo-American corporation had sought out the ANC to discuss South Africa's future must have been extremely disturbing for the National Party.

It had become clear, however, that the 'total strategy' of the government was failing. The two basic elements of this strategy were military intervention to destabilise unfriendly neighbouring states and keep a check on the ANC's military activities, and minor reforms of the apartheid system at home to encourage a supportive black middle class. By these tactics, they hoped to bring security and prosperity to white South Africa while staving off criticism and, more importantly, stiffer sanctions from the international community. The events of 1985 revealed this plan to be misguided at best.

Indeed, by 1985, the pursuit of destabilisation merely served to alienate still further the international community. A seemingly random attack on a suburb of Gaborone in Botswana (a model African democracy in the eyes of the West) while attempting to hunt down ANC guerrillas (known as Umkhonto we Sizwe) appalled Western leaders, and when Botha gave his famous 'Rubicon address' in August 1985, the world realised what most South Africans already knew. He

The following year did bring more reform. The huge cost of enforcing the pass laws, and the demands of employers for a more mobile workforce, led to their repeal in 1986. This was a welcome step forward which gave blacks greater freedom and mobility. However, even this positive act had some negative side effects. As more people moved away from their traditional homelands in search of work, they moved into areas with different political and tribal allegiances and increased the pressure on squatter camps such as Crossroads. This exacerbated the violence that had already broken out between different elements of the black population.

There had been conflict between Indians and Africans in Inanda, near Durban, in 1985. But more disturbingly, the 'black-on-black' violence between ANC and Inkatha supporters that had accompanied the revolt in 1985 began to take on the proportions of a civil war in Natal in 1986. The growing realisation on the part of ANC/UDF supporters that Inkatha and local vigilante groups were being supported by the South African police and armed forces added a particularly bitter twist to their already unhappy relationship. When the *witdoeke* (white headbands) vigilantes evicted thousands of 'squatters' from Crossroads and other squatter camps around Cape Town in May and June of 1986, the police refused to intervene and were even accused of protecting the vigilantes.

Part of the problem, particularly in Natal, was tribal. Many of the ANC's supporters came from Xhosa tribes while most of Inkatha's were Zulus, but it was not as simple as this. Many ANC were not Xhosa, and indeed there were many Zulus who were pro-ANC. Much of the violence stemmed from attempts to either topple, or maintain, petty local chiefdoms and power bases. Some saw these chiefs as collaborators in apartheid while others thought them the legitimate focus of tribal allegiances. Either way, once law and order had broken down in the spiral of violence, groups of armed young men on both sides felt genuine 'people's power' on a local level, and there

were now too many scores to settle and too much territory to defend for them to lay down their weapons.

However, the root causes of this violence lay in fundamental political differences which were a direct result of the apartheid system and could not be attributed to age-old tribal feuds. The ANC had long supported an all-inclusive ideal of South African development which involved a strong, unitary, majority-rule state, and which saw 'separate development' as an inherently racist concept which had led the nation into its present sorry state. The Zulu-dominated Inkatha represented a tradition which saw 'independent' black homelands as the best way to avoid excessive white interference. To black Africans with strong tribal traditions, 'separate development' was not necessarily objectionable, they simply wanted equality with whites and greater autonomy. As a consequence, the government often aided tribal chiefs in an attempt to maintain separateness in the face of the ANC threat.

While the violence continued in Natal and the Cape, a high-

Below: The squalid shanty town of Little Soweto near Port Elizabeth houses 120,000 blacks. High unemployment is just one of the problems faced by its inhabitants.

Right: An old man from Tsakane township near Johannesburg shows his pass book. These were used to regulate the movement of black people before their abolition in 1986.

Left: A child left homeless after fierce fighting between vigilantes and UDF comrades in Crossroads, tries to salvage what he can from the ruins and devastation.

Right: Tentative attempts at reform provoked a resurgence of right-wing opposition. Eugene Terre'Blanche, leader of the Afrikaner Resistance Movement (AWB), takes the stage after a scuffle at a Nationalist Party rally where Foreign Minister Pik Botha was due to address 3000 government supporters.

Below: Miners from the Kinross Gold Mine sing freedom songs at a commemorative rally for 177 miners who died in South Africa's biggest gold mine disaster in 1986. COSATU, and the mineworkers in particular, were one of the few effective forces of opposition to the South African government in the chaos of the late 1980s.

ranking Commonwealth delegation arrived in South Africa in an attempt to initiate negotiations. With seemingly reckless contempt for their efforts, the South African Defence Force launched air raids on the three Commonwealth capitals of Gaborone, Harare, and Lusaka. The talks were broken off, and in July a new State of Emergency was imposed. By the end of the year, 23,000 people had been detained without trial, and the only reports on the violence that the media were allowed to carry were those issued by the government.

By the summer of 1987 it was clear that revolution was not around the corner. The townships could be made ungovernable, but the UDF comrades could do little to dent seriously the considerable military power of the SADF and the police. When a group of pro-ANC guerrillas were arrested in the Western Cape in August, much of the resistance to the government crumbled. However, violence in the townships now seemed endemic. On the Witwatersrand around Johannesburg, newly-arrived Zulu hostel-dwellers and police-supported vigilantes continued to clash with comrades.

The most disciplined reformist group now seemed to be the trade unions who had been increasingly active in the UDF since the foundation of COSATU (Congress of South African Trade Unions) in 1985. In 1987 the NUM (National Union of Mineworkers) organised a successful three-week strike on the Witwatersrand gold mines, and although a black railway workers strike ended in violence, the unions survived the banning of the UDF in February 1988 to become one of the few remaining organized sources of opposition.

Through 1988 South Africa was in a state of exhausted stalemate. Sanctions had taken effect, and as the economy suffered, support for the right-wing Conservative Party grew. Archbishop Desmond Tutu provided some focus for opposition, but with most of the effective political organisations banned and a government concerned about a resurgent white right-wing, there seemed to be little hope of breaking the deadlock. But the deadlock was broken, and from an unlikely quarter — the hierarchy of the National Party itself.

It had become obvious to many in government that something had to be done to rejuvenate the economy and restore order. When the leader of the National Party in the Transvaal, F W de Klerk, proposed a meeting with the ANC in Lusaka, Botha publicly criticised him. The party had had enough. In August 1989 they forced Botha to step down as president and replaced him with de Klerk. Any change at the top had to be a move in the right direction, but there was little reason at this stage to assume that this previously staunch supporter of apartheid would prove any more sympathetic to the wishes of black South Africans than his predecessor.

THE RELEASE OF MANDELA

Frederik Willem de Klerk was steeped in the traditions of the Afrikaner nation and apartheid. His father, Jan, had served as a cabinet minister in the Verwoerd government and his uncle, J G Strijdom, was a former prime minister. After founding a successful law practice, de Klerk entered parliament in 1972 and became the youngest member of the Vorster cabinet in 1978. He had always been a strong advocate of the apartheid system, speaking out in favour of separate institutions and living areas as late as 1989, and he was the favoured presidential candidate of the right wing of the National Party.

But de Klerk did realise that the only way out of South Africa's self-destructive impasse was through meaningful dialogue with the ANC. In October 1989 the government released eight of their leaders from their life imprisonment, and in de Klerk's opening address to Parliament on 2 February

1990, he lifted the ban on the ANC, PAC and SACP. Nine days later, the world's most famous political prisoner, Nelson Mandela, was released after 27 years of imprisonment, and at last there was a glimmer of hope for reform.

Mandela had been offered his freedom in 1985 but had refused because of the condition that he renounce violence. He had been talking to the government since 1986 in an attempt to persuade them to begin negotiations with the ANC, and in July 1989 had even met P W Botha who Mandela later described as 'a charming man indeed'. Thus Mandela's release can be seen as the logical conclusion of a prolonged period of detente, but the move was still a considerable gamble for de Klerk. The growth of serious opposition on the right was shown by the Conservative Party achieving 31 per cent of the white vote in the 1989 elections, and it was not clear that there

Above: Freedom! Nelson Mandela and his wife Winnie salute well-wishers on his release from Victor Verster prison on 11 February 1990.

Left: F W de Klerk is inaugurated as the President of South Africa in September 1989. Despite his impeccable apartheid credentials, de Klerk was to launch South Africa on the road to meaningful reform.

Right: Mandela acknowledges the cheers of United Nations members in the General Assembly Hall during a speech to the UN Committee Against Apartheid in June 1990.

was a real desire for reform among the white population as a whole. There were, however, some factors which lessened the risk of the strategy. The ANC had been seriously weakened by attacks on its military bases abroad, and with the world-wide collapse of the Communist states which may have aided the ANC, de Klerk's security advisers were convinced that the organisation did not pose a serious military threat.

On his release, Mandela called for a continuation of the armed struggle until the conditions were right for a negotiated settlement, but in May 1990 the government and the ANC began talks in a cordial atmosphere, and two months after the State of Emergency was lifted in June, the ANC did agree to a ceasefire.

During the course of 1991, the government began to dismantle the apartheid system. The laws that upheld racial classifications and discrimination in land ownership, urban residence, and public segregation were removed one by one. The Land Acts (which restricted ownership of 87 per cent of the land to whites), the Group Areas Act (which specified separate residential areas for the different racial groups), The Separate Amenities Act (which controlled the use of public amenities), and the Population Registration Act (which classified the population by race) were all repealed. South Africa took its first tentative steps toward a genuinely multi-racial society.

Unfortunately, violence in the townships continued unabated. Inkatha-supporting councillors and policemen were still the main targets and 'necklacing' was commonplace. In the summer of 1990, the 'Reef War', fought by indisciplined groups of Inkatha hostel-dwellers and ANC self-defence units (SDUs), claimed the lives of 500 in an 11-day period in August. The fear of spiralling violence concentrated the minds of the politicians and led to a meeting between Mandela and Buthelezi in January 1991. Both leaders expressed a desire for peace, but the killing did not stop, and there were bitter recriminations on all sides about the role of the police in the clashes between Inkatha and ANC supporters. There were even allegations that a government-sponsored 'third force' was behind the violence.

The refusal of the police or the government to disarm Inkatha supporters of their 'traditional' Zulu weapons had long

Left: A Zulu hostel dweller is beaten and then set alight by local Xhosa residents in Soweto. Fierce fighting in August 1990 claimed the lives of 77 people in just four days.

Below left: Zulu hostel-dwellers brandish their 'traditional' weapons at a razor wire barricade which separates them from squatter areas of Alexandra township outside Johannesburg. The red headbands are to identify which side they are on during clashes with ANC comrades.

Right: Armed youths supportive of the ANC prepare for battle against Inkatha-supporting Zulus in Soweto during the summer of 1990.

rankled the ANC, but the revelations in the press of active police help for Inkatha were a severe blow to the peace process. Reports of South African military training for 200 Inkatha vigilantes were backed up by a military intelligence officer who claimed that substantial amounts of funding and weaponry had been given to Inkatha and its affiliates since 1985. In July 1991 the government was forced to admit its support for Inkatha and the reputation and integrity of de Klerk suffered a huge blow. There was clear proof that the government was pursuing a 'double agenda' of talking peace with the ANC while simultaneously supporting violent efforts to undermine it.

Mandela's previous assessment of de Klerk as a 'man of integrity' was shown to be somewhat naive, and his own reputation suffered in the eyes of many of his younger and more radical supporters. The image of Buthelezi as a collaborator in apartheid dependent upon the government was reinforced, and it was only the sheer scale of the violence that forced the leaders into a National Peace Accord in September 1991. The ANC, the government, Inkatha, and a number of church, trade union, business, and homeland leaders put their name to the agreement. In December, 19 political parties came together in the Convention for a Democratic South Africa (Codesa) to discuss a new South African constitution.

Above: Nelson Mandela, President de Klerk and Inkatha leader Mangosuthu Buthelezi have time for a smile after signing the National Peace Accord on 14 September 1991 in an attempt to end the township warfare.

Right: A woman shifts through the remains of her shack in Katlehong after it was destroyed by residents of a neighbouring camp during an attack on the township.

While Codesa's working groups were attempting to thrash out the details of an interim constitution, the National Party lost their second by-election to the Conservative Party in three months. De Klerk decided to take another huge risk in an attempt to head off criticism from the right and provide his government with a mandate for reform. He announced a whites-only referendum on the peace process for March 1992. A defeat would probably have led to civil war, but 68 per cent gave their support in a high turnout. In the two-and-a-half years since de Klerk had come to power progress had been slow, and often acrimonious, but with the formal approval of the whites, it seemed that the most serious barrier to reform had finally been removed. Mandela and de Klerk seemed ready to usher in a new era in South Africa.

THE PATH TO REFORM

In the early spring of 1992, there were genuine grounds for optimism about South Africa's future. Some of the economic sanctions were removed in response to the real, if slow, progress toward reform; South Africa's athletes were preparing for a return to the world sporting arena at the Barcelona Olympics; and most importantly, de Klerk had just received his mandate for reform from the whites. But the Codesa negotiations were not going smoothly. Fundamental differences between the ANC and the government over the nature and timing of the new constitution came to a head in May and the talks were broken off.

The two sides could not even agree on the basic ground rules for decision-making procedures, and it became clear to the ANC that the government was in no hurry to thrash out a deal. De Klerk's position was now secure within his own constituency, and not surprisingly he had no desire to rush headlong into a new constitution which would inevitably lead to a diminished role for himself and his party.

The dynamics of the situation would not allow the government to stall indefinitely, however. The death toll since the signing of the National Peace Accord in September 1991 was 1500, and radical young ANC activists resented their leaders talking to the very people they held responsible for these deaths. ANC leaders devised a plan of 'mass action' to force the issue and staged a well-organised 'stayaway' on 16 June, the anniversary of Soweto. The event was overshadowed, however, by an incident of horrific brutality the following day in Boipatong.

Hostel-dwellers rampaged through the township hacking, stabbing and shooting 45 people to death. The attack lasted over four hours, giving credibility to accusations that the police were accomplices. To make matters worse, a demonstration two days later protesting against the massacre was fired on by the police killing three more. Mandela had little option but to suspend talks with the government until it demonstrated a genuine desire to control its police and armed forces.

Evidence of 'dirty tricks' and military support for Inkatha had been mounting steadily. In April, a white police officer had been found guilty of participating in the murder of 11 ANC supporters (including six women and two children) four years previously. In May, concrete evidence emerged that the killing of four leading black activists in 1985 had been carried out at the behest of military intelligence. The revelations added to the atmosphere of grass-roots outrage, and with feelings running high, a supposedly peaceful march on the Ciskei capital Bisho ended with disastrous results.

The Ciskei homeland was ruled rather uneasily by the military dictator Oupa Gqozo. It was seen as a weak link in the homeland system, and many in the ANC hoped that a show of strength would convert Ciskei troops and police to their cause. When the march reached the border, a small group of demonstrators saw what seemed to be an unguarded gap in the

Left: The brutal massacre of 45 people in Boipatong in June 1992 was shocking even by South African standards. Here mourners grieve over the coffin of a victim of the most horrific single incident in the reform era.

Above right: Tens of thousands of ANC supporters marched on Bisho, the capital of Ciskei, in an attempt to occupy the city and inspire its people to overthrow their leader Oupa Gqozo. The march ended in disaster when 28 were killed by the Ciskeian Defence Force.

Right: One of the most dramatic symbols of South Africa's gradual reincorporation into the international fold was their appearance at the 1992 Barcelona Olympics.

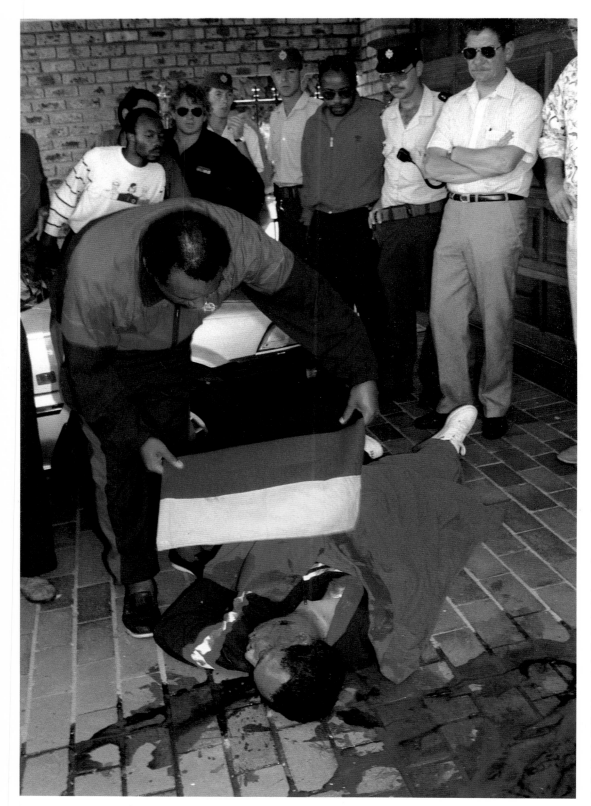

Left: The assassination of the popular ANC and SACP leader Chris Hani threatened to derail the peace process. ANC executive Tokyo Sexwale covers Hani's body with an ANC flag shortly after he was shot in a white suburb of Johannesburg on 10 April 1993.

Above right: Demonstrators crouch behind a car as police open fire in Soweto. After attending a rally to mourn the death of Chris Hani, thousands of demonstrators laid siege to the township's police station.

Right: This picture of demonstrators gathered outside the Rand Supreme Court to greet three alleged co-conspirators in Hani's murder shows the considerable depth of feeling aroused by his assassination.

fences surrounding a stadium which would have given them a route into the nearby centre of Bisho. Unfortunately this 'gap' was defended by Ciskei troops lying in trenches, who opened fire on the charging demonstrators killing 28.

The double tragedies of Boipatong and Bisho were not the only embarrassment for the government. In an attempt to placate growing international and domestic concern, de Klerk had appointed Justice Goldstone to investigate the allegations of 'third force' activity and to examine the root causes of the violence. The report of the Goldstone Commission exonerated the government from direct involvement in planning the violence and argued that the root cause was ANC/Inkatha rivalry, but it was highly critical of security force transgres-

sions. The clear message was that the government had not exercised sufficient control over powerful rogue elements within the security system. The government were also criticised for not implementing previous recommendations to ban the carrying of weapons and remove the notoriously brutal 32 Battalion from the townships.

Economic recession, drought, and rampant corruption added to the woes of South Africa at the end of 1992, but faced with a desperate situation, the politicians once again realised that compromise and dialogue were the only solution. A Record of Understanding was signed in September, and de Klerk agreed to bans on weapons, new security measures for the hostels, and a purge of the police and armed forces to remove the most reactionary elements. In turn, the ANC seemed more willing to tone down their demands for an immediate majority-rule government, offering the prospect of power sharing after an election.

By April 1993 the multi-party talks had resumed with an even greater number of parties present than at the last round. Among the new participants were the Zulu King Goodwill Zwelethini, the PAC, the Conservative Party and other white right-wingers from the Afrikaner Volksunie. Only days after they began, South Africa was rocked by the assassination of Chris Hani, a popular ANC leader with a huge following

among young blacks. Hani, a former guerrilla commander, was the head of Umkhonto and a passionate orator. He had been converted to the process of negotiation and was one of the few leaders who could effectively control the ANC's unruly township activists. His murder by a white assassin in a white suburb of Johannesburg threatened to derail the peace process once again, and might have done so, had not Mandela appealed for calm and channelled the outrage into largely peaceful and disciplined protests.

The frustration of black South Africa at the pace of reform — it was now three years since Mandela's release — was threatening to brim over once again, but by his impartial, statesman-like behaviour and his reassurances to the whites, Mandela not only gained moral authority, but made white South Africa realise they needed his steadying influence if they were to avert even greater chaos.

The talks now took on a more pronounced bilateral nature, with the ANC and National Party dictating the terms to the other parties. The liberal-minded Democratic Party managed to provide some restraints during the negotiations, but Inkatha, the only other party with sufficient support to be capable of this, walked out of the talks in July after the election date of April 1994 was agreed upon and the first draft of an interim constitution was drawn up.

Buthelezi objected to the election of a constituent assembly and wanted the constitution written before the election to prevent a landslide ANC victory allowing them to write it on their own. He also objected to the proposed status of KwaZulu/Natal (which the ANC proposed to call simply Natal) and argued for a far greater degree of federalism. As his support was pre-

dominantly regional, he knew Inkatha's best chance of meaningful power was to gain control of a largely autonomous KwaZulu/Natal, and he feared its subjegation in an ANC-governed unitary state.

The basic philosophy behind this dissent was shared by the far-right parties, who had by now banded together as the Afrikaner Volksfront (AVF) under General Viljoen. No one was quite sure where the projected Afrikaner *volkstaat* that they advocated would actually be, but this did not stop the AVF from joining forces with Inkatha and the black homeland leaders in August to form the 'Freedom Alliance'. Determined to press for a federal state, they threatened to boycott the elections and made dark predictions of civil war.

The promised interim constitution did incorporate some elements of federalism. As well as a National Assembly elected by proportional representation, there would be elected regional legislatures which in turn would elect South Africa's new Senate. The leading players offered some concessions to Buthelezi in August but refused to be sidetracked by his rejection. In any case, there was still much to be agreed upon by the ANC and the government.

The two main stumbling blocks were the government's insistence that the cabinet (in which all parties with a certain minimum support would have members) take decisions by a two-thirds majority, and the ANC's desire for new elections immediately after the adoption of the new constitution. In intense negotiations just hours before the final plenary session on 17 November, the government gave way on the former, agreeing to 'a consensus-seeking spirit' in decision making, and the ANC gave way on the latter, agreeing to a fixed five-year period of power-sharing before the next election.

After an exhausting seven months of negotiations, agreement on an interim constitution had finally been reached. It was not too soon either, South Africa's endemic violence had shown no signs of abating, and, if anything, became worse during 1993. The 'Reef War' had broken out again on the Witwatersrand, claiming well over 1000 lives over the year, and even more were killed in Natal. Atrocities and outrages were perpetrated on all sides. As 1993 drew to a close there was genuine relief and jubilation at the breakthrough, but everyone knew the troubles were not over yet.

Above: Lucas Mangope of Bophuthatswana (second from left), Oupa Gqoza of Ciskei (centre), and Chief Buthelezi of KwaZulu (right) were the three most important black leaders in the Freedom Alliance. The two homeland leaders and Buthelezi joined forces with the white right to defend their independence and promote the idea of a loose federation for the new South Africa.

Left: Nelson Mandela and F W de Klerk jointly received the Nobel Peace Prize in December 1993. Relations between the two men were notably strained by this point, but they had managed to retain a basic respect for each other.

THE YEAR OF THE ELECTIONS

As the elections approached, a Transitional Executive Council (TEC), dominated by the ANC and the government, tried to ensure the conditions necessary for their success. Their main concern was the continuing refusal of the Freedom Alliance to take part in the elections, and of particular concern was Inkatha's intransigence and the threats of white extremists like Eugene Terre'Blanche of the neo-nazi AWB.

The rhetoric of Buthelezi was becoming increasingly confrontational, and although the National Party seemed mildly sympathetic to his demands for greater autonomy for KwaZulu/Natal, few in the ANC seemed willing to bring Buthelezi back on side. Opinion polls showed Buthelezi's support to be slipping, his reputation having suffered from his obstructive stance and his rather sordid alliance with white extremists, and it seemed likely that Inkatha might not even win control of the KwaZulu/Natal legislature. At the end of 1993, many in the ANC were quite prepared to let their traditional enemy go its own way and then bring down all the military power of the state on Inkatha after the election should it refuse to abide by the results.

But by February 1994, although the ANC were still determined that the election take place as scheduled, they realised that some concessions had to be made if they were to avoid civil war. The unholy alliance of Inkatha, the AVF, and homeland leaders such as Gqozu in Ciskei and Lucas Mangope in Bophuthatswana, would not be capable of overthrowing the

Above: Mandela in a jovial mood on the campaign trail in the run-up to South Africa's first mutli-racial elections. Wrapped in a blanket, he finds time for a dance during his visit to Sasolburg in the Orange Free State.

Left: After their attempt to prevent the ousting of Bophuthatswanan leader Lucas Mangope by his own people, these neo-nazi AWB members are trapped by the Bophuthatswana police. The man crouching with his hands up was shot dead moments after this picture was taken.

South African government, but they could wage a bloody guerrilla war that might drag on for years. And if the prospect of trying to crush the sprawling, warren-like townships and remote hilly hinterlands of KwaZulu was not daunting enough in itself, the ANC also faced the prospect of an Afrikaner uprising. Mandela thought the white extremists to be genuinely powerful and knew that relying on the security services to defeat their former colleagues in order to protect a black-majority government was extremely risky. Consequently, he felt more inclined to placate the AVF than he did their black allies.

The leader of the AVF, General Viljoen, had experienced the horrors of guerrilla war in Angola, Mozambique, and Namibia, and did not with to see them in South Africa. He was prepared to participate in the election in exchange for an Afrikaner council which would examine the possibility of obtaining a *volkstaat* by constitutional means. Unfortunately, the AVF rejected Viljoen's proposals and as the first deadline for party registration passed, the main elements of the Freedom Alliance stood firm in their refusal to participate in the elections.

On 16 February the ANC announced a package of constitutional concessions which they hoped would defuse the situation. They included increased powers for the provincial governments with guarantees that these powers would survive in the new constitution, double ballot papers (which were thought to favour smaller, regional parties), a principle of internal self-determination, a 20-member Akrikaner council to discuss the feasibility of a *volkstaat*, and the renaming of Natal as KwaZulu/Natal.

Rather than giving the proposals careful consideration and consulting with his allies, Buthelezi, who had declared KwaZulu independent two days earliers, rushed to condemn them. A final deadline for party registration of 4 March was set and the nation waited anxiously to see if the Freedom Alliance would register for the elections or send South Africa on the path to civil war. Three days before the deadline, Mandela met Buthelezi in a last ditch attempt to avert disaster, and promises of international mediation persuaded Buthelezi to 'provisionally' register his party. In response, Viljoen, acting on his own initiative, registered a new party, the Freedom Front, minutes before the deadline, to keep the door open for the far-right as well. But he was later castigated by a meeting of the AVF who were determined not to participate.

Meanwhile, tensions were reaching crisis point in Bophuthatswana. Worried about their future, and wanting to be part of the forthcoming elections and the new South Africa, the people of the homeland went on strike and became involved in increasingly violent clashes with Bophuthatswana police and troops. They demanded the reincorporation of Bophuthatswana into South Africa and the removal of Mangope. Despite vigorous attempts by his former friends in the South African government to persuade him to resign (and his obvious lack of real support) Mangope refused to go or to allow preparations for the elections. In a desperate attempt to maintain his grip on power in the face of mounting violence and the defection of police officers and ministers, Mangope called on his new friends in the AVF for help. He was prepared to see white racists put down a rebellion of his own people in order to stay in power.

Unfortunately, as well as troops mustered by the AVF, mobs of ill-disciplined AWB also descended on the Bophuthatswana town of Mmabatho at the behest of Terre'Blanche. The episode ended in a violent fiasco as the AWB, ordered to leave by AVF leaders and white officers of the Bophuthatswana Defence Force, went on the rampage shooting indiscriminately into the crowd. One of their vehicles was trapped by local troops and its occupants dragged out and shot by a black policeman

Left: Zulus brandishing clubs and spears attend a demonstration in Pretoria to hear their king, Goodwill Zwelethini.

Above: Blacks from the township of Katlehong wait in line at a polling station to vote in South Africa's first multi-racial elections.

in full view of the world's press as they begged for mercy. An embarrassed AVF pulled out later in the day, and Mangope was a spent force. The government, frustrated by his continuing inability to grasp the reality of the situation, lost patience with him and forced him to step down two days later.

The far-right was both split and discredited by this episode. Despite the wishes of the AVF, Viljoen decided to enter a list of candidates for his new party, effectively confirming his participation in the election, and the perception of the AWB as a serious threat had been shattered by their ridiculous and unruly behaviour.

Inkatha, however, were still a major headache for the TEC. Buthelezi had failed to register his list of candidates by 11 March, thereby allowing his earlier 'provisional' registration to lapse. Violence in Natal was escalating once more, and Buthelezi was making increasing use of the Zulu king, Goodwill Zwelethini, to mobilise the deep tribal loyalty of the Zulu people. While many Zulus regretted the descent of this figurehead into party politics, it did help to strengthen opposition to the ANC and the new constitution.

After the head of the Independent Electoral Commission (IEC), Judge Kriegler, was humiliated by the KwaZulu legislature while attempting to secure cooperation in holding the election, the situation became even worse. The ANC decided to stage a march in Durban to show their strength in Natal, and while this was relatively peaceful, Inkatha's response in Johannesburg three days later ended in running battles through the city centre after ANC supporters had fired on the march. Over 50 people were killed, some of them shot by ANC employees outside their headquarters in Shell House.

Whether the demonstrators were really trying to storm the building or not, Mandela and the ANC came in for severe criticism, and the belief of Inkatha that the ANC were determined to crush them was reinforced.

Three days later, on 31 March, Natal was once again placed under a State of Emergency as the IEC tried to show its determination for the election to proceed. But with Buthelezi declaring the start of 'the final struggle to the finish between the ANC and the Zulu nation', and with violent electoral intimidation rife, the chances of genuinely free and fair elections in Natal were remote, even if Inkatha could be persuaded to participate.

However, the international mediation promised by Mandela failed to get off the ground. The two sides could not agree on whether the postponement of the election was to be included in the talks, and Buthelezi was beginning to run out of options. He was now heavily dependent on the King's support if he was to mount effective opposition to the new regime, and the breakthrough eventually came after the King had been successfully isolated from Buthelezi with offers of an entrenched constitutional position for the Zulu monarchy.

Realising that he could lose everything, with only one week to go before the election, Buthelezi capitulated and agreed to take part, claiming unconvincingly that the concessions offered to the King had satisfied his demands. Frantic last-minute campaigning followed, and the with help of some hastily produced stickers, the name of the Inkatha Freedom Party finally took its place on the ballot sheets for South Africa's first free multi-racial elections.

The election itself was remarkably peaceful given the horrific violence that had occurred in the previous decade. Its organisation was often rather shambolic, with allegations of vote-rigging, and there was queuing for three days or more at many polling stations, but it was pronounced 'substantially free and fair' by the IEC, and most international observers agreed.

As expected, the ANC achieved an outright victory, capturing 62.6 per cent of the votes and 252 seats in the 400-seat

Right: ANC supporters celebrate their victory in the 1994 elections. The ANC received nearly 63 per cent of the vote and gained control of six of the nine provincial assemblies.

Below: Nelson Mandela takes the oath of office to become the first black president of South Africa at the age of 75.

National Assembly, and taking overall control of six of the nine provincial assemblies. But there was significant support for the National Party among the white and Coloured population. They gained 82 seats in the National Assembly with 20.4 per cent of the vote and took control of the Western Cape with 53.2 per cent. Inkatha returned 43 members to the National Assembly with 10.5 per cent, and against most pundits' expectations, they just scraped home in KwaZulu/Natal with 41 of the 81 seats.

No other party received significant support on a National level. The Freedom Front managed just over 2 per cent of the poll, the Democratic Party could only muster 1.7 per cent, and the PAC received a meagre 1.5 per cent of the votes.

In many respects it was a happy result. The ANC had their victory, but not the two-thirds majority which would have allowed them to write the constitution on their own. Thus the whites and other minorities were somewhat reassured. More importantly, perhaps, Inkatha gained control of KwaZulu/Natal. This will undoubtedly raise fears among the non-Zulu population, but at least this result reduces the prospect of insurrection in the province by giving Inkatha a real stake in the new South Africa.

On 10 May 1994 Mandela was duly inaugurated as president after his election by the new members of the National Assembly. Under the interim constitution any party receiving over 20 per cent of the votes could nominate a deputy president and so de Klerk took his place in the new government as one of the two deputy presidents alongside the well-respected Thabo Mbeki, the ANC National Chairman. Included in Mandela's Government of National Unity are six ministers from the National Party and three ministers from Inkatha, with Buthelezi as the Minister of Home Affairs.

Mandela's government has had many problems in trying to implement its programme of reform, not least sluggish economic growth which is barely keeping pace with the growth in population, and an alien and complex bureaucratic system. During the election, the ANC promised an ambitious programme of land redistribution, house building, affirmative action for all non-whites, free primary health care for children under six and pregnant mothers, and compulsory free state education. However, it was clear after four months in office that the new government had not acquired full control of the machinery of state. Many ministers admitted to having little idea of how their departments operated, and Mandela himself has conceded that 'the wheels of government grind slowly'. In its first 100 days in office the new government, by its own admission, had yet to tackle the fundamental structural changes it pledged itself to address.

Yet given the enormity of their task this is perhaps not surprising. The mere fact that South Africa has avoided the violent pitfalls that many thought it would succumb to is to be applauded. There has been a dramatic reduction in violence in KwaZulu/Natal as ANC and Inkatha cabinet ministers have shown an exemplary willingness to co-operate in the Inkatha-led joint administration. The violence still continues in many places but on a much smaller scale, and the far-right backlash that many feared has yet to materialise. In these terms, Mandela's government has started well, but the real challenge is to encourage the investment needed for economic growth. For without this, the government will find it difficult to carry out the ambitious programmes its supporters expect, and deserve, after their long history of oppression.

INDEX

Figures in *italics* refer to illustrations.

Active Citizen Force 121, 132, 172
African National Congress (ANC) 118, 138-39, *139*, 148, 152, 168, 170, 172, *172*, *173*, 174, *174*, 178, 186-206
Afrikaner Bond 57, *57*, 84, 90
Afrikaner Party 142, 153
Afrikaner Resistance Movement (AWB) *191*, 203, *203*, 204-5
Afrikaner Volksfront (AVF) 202-5
Afrikaners
  apartheid 159, 182
  1920s 134, 136
  Rebellion (1914) 120-21
  Republic 162, 164, 165
  Second Anglo-Boer War, aftermath 111, 112
  Second World War 140, 141
  Smuts, Jan Christiaan 122, 124
  Union of South Africa 118
  see also Boers
agriculture
  early settlers 14, 15, 16, 17,
  Great Trek, origins of 28
  post-Second Anglo-Boer War 111, *111*, 112
  post-First World War 134, 136
  post-Second World War 150, 152, 153
Air Force, South African (SAAF)
  Second World War 145
  Mozambique 178
Anglo-Boer Wars
  First 73, 75-76, *75-81*, 78-80, 87
  Second 80, 92-95, *92-110*, 97, 100, 103-10, *122*
Angola 16, 121, 168, 174, 179
  civil war 167-68, 175, *175-78*, 176, 178, 180
Anstruther, Lieutenant-Colonel 76
apartheid 118, *137*, 138, 153, *163*
  introduction of legislation 156, *156*, 158-59
  implementation 160-62, *160-62*
  resistance 170, *170-74*, 172, 174
  reform 182, 184, *184*, *185*, 186-206
arms embargo (1977) 168
assassination attempts on Dr Verwoerd 164, *164*, 166, *167*

Baden-Powell, Colonel Robert *102*, 103
Bantu people 10, 12, 25, 27
Barcelona Olympics (1992) 198, *199*
Basutoland *see* Lesotho
Batavia 14, 15, 19
Beach, Sir Michael Hicks 75, *75*
Bechuanaland *see* Botswana
Beit, Alfred 55, 82, *82*, 88, *88*, 90
Beyers, Commandant-General Christian 120, *121*
Biko, Steve 174, *174*
Bisho 198, *199*, 200
Black Consciousness movement 174
Black Week 97
blacks in South Africa, 20th century situation
  aftermath of Boer War 111-12
  franchise question (1908) 116-17
  Native Land Act (1913) 118
  First World War 128, 129, 131, post- labour problems 132, 134, 136
  Native bills (1926) 138
  Second World War 147-48, post- labour problems 150, *150-51*, 152-53
  see also African National Congress, apartheid, Black Consciousness movement, homelands, nationalism, Pan African Congress, pass laws, Sharpeville massacre (1960), Soweto unrest (1976)
Bloemfontein 46, *48*, 95, 97, 100, *101*, 104, *110*, 116, *139*
Blood River, Battle of (1838) 23-24, 33, 38-39, *38-41*, 73
Boers *28*, *29*, 64
  Anglo-Boer Wars, First 73, 75-76, 78-80, *75-81*, 87, Second 80, 92-95, *92-110*, 97, 100, 103-10, *123*
  Durban, arrival in 23-24
  Great Trek 28-39, *30-41*
  Natal, annexation of 42-44
  1914 Rebellion 120-21, *120*
  Republics 45-48, 60
  see also Afrikaners, Kruger
Botha, General Louis 97, 105, 106, 107, 109, 110, 111, *112*, 116, *117*, 118, 122, 125, *125*, 126, *127*, 134
Boipatong 198, *198*, 200
Bophuthatswana 203, *203*, 204, 205
Botha, P W 168, 182, *182*, 184, *185*, 186, 187, 191, 192
Botha, 'Pik' 168
Botswana (formerly Bechuanaland) 87, 166, 167, 168, 187
Bower, Sir Graham 90
Brazzaville agreement (1988) 180
British
  Anglo-Boer Wars, First 73, 75-6, *75-81*, 78-80, 87, Second 80, 92-95, *92-110*, 100, 103-10, *123*
  Boer republics 45-46
  Cape, takeover of 19, *19-21*, 21
  Durban, arrival in 22-24
  Imperial Conference (1926) 138
  Jameson Raid (1895) 74, 88-89, *90*, 91, *91*
  Natal, annexation of 42-44, *43*
  Republic, formation of 163-65
  Transvaal, annexation of 60, *60-63*, 63, 64, 73, 75, 84, return of 79, 80
  Union, creation of 116-18
  Zulu War 64-65, *65-72*, 68, 70-72
British South Africa Company (BSA) 87, *87*, 88, 90
Buller, General Sir Redvers 95, *95*, 97, 100, 103, 106
burghers
  early settlers 15, *15*, 17, 18, 19
  First Anglo-Boer War 76, 79
  Second Anglo-Boer War 92, 94, 100, 103, 105, 107, 109, 110
  1914 Rebellion 120, *120*
Burgers, Thomas François 60, *60*
bus boycotts *151*, 152
Buthelezi, Chief Mangosuthu 195, 196, *196*, 201-6
Butler, Sir William 87, 93

Cape Colony 57, 60, 82, 95, 122
  British takeover 19, *19-21*, 21
  Cecil Rhodes 84, 87
  Coloured electoral divisions 159
  diamonds, effect of 52, 55
  early settlers 10, 14-17, *18*, 49, 73
  Great Trek from 31, *31*
  Natal, annexation to 43-44
  native bills 138
  Second Anglo-Boer War 100, 106, 107, 109, 112
  Transvaal, support for 75
Cape Town 17, *64*, *85*, 95, *105*, *113*, 116, *118*, *184*
Carnarvon, Lord 60, *63*, 75
Cetshwayo, Zulu king 64, *64*, 65, 68, 70, *70*, 72
Chamberlain, Joseph 73, 88, *89*, 90, 91, 92
Chelmsford, Lieutenant-General Lord 64, *64*, 68, 70, 71, 72
China 12
  indentured labourers in gold mines *111*, 112
Chissano, Joachim 178
Churchill, Winston 124, *124*
Cilliers, Sarel 38, *38*
Ciskei 198, *199*, 200, 203
Coalition Government (1933) 139
Colenso, Battle of (1899) *96*, 97, *98*
Coloureds 139
  First World War 131
  franchise question (1908) 116-17
  improvement of constitutional position, 1970s 182, 184
  political rights bill (1926) 138
  Race Classification Board 156
  resistance to apartheid 170, 172, 186
  Second World War 147
Commonwealth 153, 163-64, 165
Communism 132, 139, *139*, *152*, 170, *170*
concentration camps, Second Anglo-Boer War 107, 108, *108*
Congress of Democrats 170
Congress of the People 170
Congress of South African Trade Unions (COSATU) *190*, 191
Conservative Party (Dr Treurnicht's) 184, 191, 192, 196, 201
Convention for a Democratic South Africa (Codesa) 196, 198
Cresswell, Colonel Frank 134
Cronje, General Piet 76, 100, *100*, 103
Crossroads *186*, 188, *190*
Cry the Beloved Country (novel and film) *162*, *170*
Cuban troops in Angola 175, 178, 180

Da Gama, Vasco 12, *13*
Dabulamanzi, Zulu chief 64, *65*, 68
De Beers companies 52, 55, 84, 87
de Klerk, F W *188*, 191, 192, *192*, 195-206
de la Rey, General 95, 103, 105, 109, 111, *112*, 120
de Wet, General Christiaan 100, *101*, 103, 105, *107*, 110, *112*, 120, 121, *121*
Delville Wood, Battle of (1916) 130, *130-31*
Dhaklama, Alfonso 178
diamond mines 52, *52-54*, 55, 57, *57*, 82, 84, *84*, 94, *135*
Dias de Novaes, Bartolomeu 12, *12*
Dingane, Zulu king 22, *22*, 23, 24, 27, 34, *34*, *35*, 38, 39, 42
Dingiswayo, Mthethwa chief 25, 27
Dominion Party 139
Drake, Francis 14
Dube, Reverend John L 111, *112*
Durban 22-24, *22*, *24*, 31, 33, 34, 42, 43, 94, 116
  Indian immigrants 49, *49-51*
d'Urban, Major General Sir Benjamin 23, *23*
Dutch East India Company 14-16, 18, 19

East Africa
  First World War 122, 128-29, 131
  Second World War 143, *143*, *144*, 145
economy
  1920s 136, 1930s 139, Second World War 148, post- 150, 152-53,
  Commonwealth, effect of withdrawal from 165,
  1960s 167, 1970s 184,
  present situation 186
elections, General
  (1924) 132, (1929) 139, (1943) 153, (1948) *138*, 153, 156, 160, (1958) *160*, (1989) 192, (1994) 203-6

First World War
  Delville Wood, Battle of (1916) 130, *130-31*
  East African Campaign (1915-18) 122, 128-29, *128-29*, 131
  Egypt 130
  France 130-31, *130-31*
  South West Africa Campaign (1915) *114-15*, 120, 125-26, *125-27*, 131
Fischer, Abraham 116
FNLA movement, Angola, 175
Fourie, Jopie 121, 141
France 166
  First World War 130-31, *130-31*
  Huguenots, arrival of 16
franchise question (1908) 116-17
Freedom Alliance 202, 204
Freedom Front 204-6
Frelimo movement, Mozambique, 178
Frontier Wars
  Fourth (1811-12) 19
  Sixth (1834-35) 28, *46*
  Seventh – 'War of the Axe' *47*
  Eighth (1850-53) 45, *47*
Fynn, Henry Francis 22, *22*

Gandhi, Mahatma 51, *51*, 111, 117
Gardiner, Captain Allan Francis 22, *22*
General Strike (1922) 132, *133*
Germans in Africa
  early settlers in the Cape 15, 16, 73
  South West African Campaign (1915) 120, 125-26, *125-27*
  East African Campaign (1915-18) 128-29, *129*
  North African Campaign (1941-42) 144, 145
Gladstone, William 73, 75
gold 132, 136, 139, 162, 165
gold mining *55*, 74, 82-83, *83*, 111, 112
  Chinese indentured labourers *111*, 112
  strikes (1907) 116, (1946) *150*, 152
Goldstone Commission 200
Gqozo, Oupa 198, *202*, 203
Great Depression 139
Great Trek 28-39, *28-41*, 73
Griquas people 45, 52
Group Areas Act (1950) 156, 195
Gumede, Joseph 139

Hani, Chris *200*, 201, *201*
Hare, Colonel John *47*
Havenga, N C 142
Hendrickse, Rev Allan 184
Hertzog, Dr Albert 182
Hertzog, J B M 118, *118*, 124, 134, 136, 138, *138*, 139, 140, 141, 142
Hobhouse, Emily 108, *108*
Hofmeyr, J H 57, 84, 117, *117*
homelands 161-62, 184, 188
Hottentots *see* Khoikhoi
Houphouet-Boigny, President Félix of Ivory Coast 167
Huguenots 16, 21

Independent Electoral Commission (IEC) 205
India 12, 14, 136, 163
Indian Congress 170
Indians in South Africa
  apartheid *158*, 170, 172, 186
  East African Campaign (1915-18) 131
  franchise question (1908) 116-17
  House of Delegates 184, 186
  immigrants in Natal 49, *49-51*, 51, 111
  1920s situation 136
  Second World War 147, post- 153
Industrial and Commercial Workers Union (ICU) 138-39
Inkatha movement 188, *194*, 195, 196, 198, 200, 201, 202-6
Isandhlwana, Zulu *impis* at (1879) 64, 65, *65*, *66-67*, 68, 71
Italy, Second World War 143, *146-49*, 147-48

Jabavu, J T 111, *112*, 118
Jameson, Dr Leander Starr 88, *88*, 89, 90, *90*, 91
Jameson Raid (1895) 74, 87, 88-89, *90*, 91, *91*, 92, 94, 122
Johannesburg 83, *83*, 89, 103, *119*, *120*, *133*, *159*, *162*, 164, *168*, 205
Joint Planning Council 170
Joubert, Commandant Frans 76, 80
Joubert, General Piet 74, 75, 76, *77*, *80*, 94

Kaunda, President Kenneth of Zambia *168*
Kemp, General 120, 121
Khoikhoi people *1*, 10, *10*, *11*, 12, *14*, 15, 16, 21, 36
Khoisan people 10, *10*, *11*, *29*
Kimberley diamond mines 52, *53*, *56*, 82, 84, *84*, *135*
  siege of 87, *87*, 94, 103, relief of 95, 100
King, Dick 'Ride' 42-43, *42*
Kitchener, Lord 97, *99*, 100, 105, 106, 107, 108, 109
Klopper, Major General 144, 145
Kok, Adam 45, *45*, 52
Kruger, President Paul 48, 60, 73-74, *73*, *74*, 75, 79, 82, 88, 89, 91, 92, 93, 100, 103, 106, *107*, 112, *113*, 122
KwaZulu 201, 202, 203, 204, 206

labour
  diamond mines 57
  gold, discovery of 82
  post-Second Anglo-Boer War 111-12
  1920s unrest 132, *133*, 134, 136
  Second World War 148, post- 150, *150-52*, 152-53
  1960s 162
Labour Party 134, 136, 139, 153
Labour Party (Rev Allan Henricke's) 184
Ladysmith, siege of (1899) 94, *94*, 95, 103, relief of (1900) 97, 100, *100*
Land Acts 195
Lanyon, Colonel Owen 75, 76, *76*
Leabua, Chief Jonathan 166, *166*
Lesotho (formerly Basutoland) 166, *166*, 168
Liberals 170
Louis, Prince Imperial of France 71-72, *72*
Lukin, Brigadier-General H T 125, 130

Machel, President Samora of Mozambique 167, 178, *178*
MacMillan, Harold 163-64, *163*, 165, 166
Madagascar, Second World War 143
Mafeking, siege of (1899) *93*, 94, relief of (1900) *102*, 103
Magersfontein, Battle of *96*, 97
Majuba, Battle of (1881) 73, 80, *80-81*, 84, 91, 92, 94
Malan, Dr D F 136, *137*, *138*, 139, 140, 141, 142, *152*, 153, 156, 158, 159
Malawi 166, 168
Mandela, Nelson 172, *173*, 192-206
Mandela, Winnie *193*
Mangope, Lucas *200*, 203, 204
Maritz, Gert 31, 33
Mashonaland 87
Matabeleland 87
Mbeki, Thabo 208
Methuen, Lieutenant-General Lord 95, 109, *110*
Milner, Sir Alfred 73, 92, *92*, 93, 106, 107, 109, 111, 112, 116
miners *54*, *55*, *56*, 57, *135*
  Chinese indentured labourers *111*, 112
  labour unrest, 1920s 132, 134
  post-Second World War 150
  strikes (1907) 116, (1913) 118, *119*, 122, (1922) 132, *133*, (1946) *150*, 152
  see also diamond mines, gold mining
Moshweshwe, Basuto leader 45, *46*
Mozambique 60, 74, 166, 167, 168, 178
Mpande, Zulu chief *44*, 64
MPLA movement, Angola 168, 175-80, *175*
Mthethwa tribe 25, 27
Muldergate scandal (1978) 182, *182*

Nairobi 128, *129*
Namibia 172, 179-80, *180*
  see also South West Africa
Napier, Sir George 24, *24*, 42, 45
Natal 10, 23, 60, 84, 111, 112, 188, 201, 202, 204, 106
  Cape Colony, annexation to 43-44
  First Anglo-Boer War 76, 79
  Great Trek 30, 31, 33, 34, 39
  Indian immigrants 49, *49-51*, 51, 111, 153
  naming of by da Gama 12
  Republic, against creation of 164
  Second Anglo-Boer War 95, 97, 103, *104*, 106, 107, 109
  sugar *135*
  Zulu War 64, 68, 70, 72
Natalia, Republic of 34, 42-43
National Party 159, 160, *160*, 163, 170, 184, 187, 191, 192, 196, 201, 203, 206 *see also* Nationalist Party
National Peace Accord (1991) 196, 198
National People's Party 184
National Union of Mineworkers (NUM) *190*, 191

nationalism, African 164
  rise of blacks in South Africa
    170, *170-74*, 172, 174, 186-
    206
Nationalist Party 124, 132, 134,
  138-39, 140, 141, 142, 153,
  see also National Party
Native bills (1926) 138
Natives Land Act (1913) 118
Navy, South African (SAN)
  Second World War 145
Nazi sympathies 140-41, *141*, *183*,
  184
Ndebele tribe 31, *32*, 33, 34
  rebellion 87
Ndongeni, Zulu retainer 43, *43*
Ndwandwe tribe 25, 27
Nigeria 166
North Africa, Second World War
  143, 144, *144-45*, 145, 147
Nujoma, Sam 180

Orange Free State 60, 116, 142
  creation of 46, 48
  diamonds, discovery of 52
  Indians not permitted residence
    51
  Republic, in favour of 164
  Second Anglo-Boer War 92, 95,
    100, *104*, 105, 110
  Transvaal, support for 75, 90
Orange River Colony 112
Orange River Sovereignty 45-46
Organisation of African Unity 166, *179*
Ossewabrandwag (Oxwagon
  Sentinel movement) (OB)
  140-41, *183*, 184

Paardeberg, Battle of (1900) 100,
  102, 103
Pan African Congress (PAC) 170,
  172, *172*, 174, 192, 201, 206
pass laws 150, *157*, 158, 170, *171*,
  172, 182, 187, *189*
Paton, Alan *162*, 170, *170*
Penn-Symons, Sir William 94
People's Party 140
People's Liberation Army of
  Namibia (PLAN) 179, 180, *180*
Pirow, Oswald *141*
Pomeroy-Colley, Major-General Sir
  George 79, *79*, 80
Population Registration Act 195
Portuguese in Angola 175, East
  Africa 31, 129, Mozambique
  60, 166, South Africa 12, *12*,
  13, 14, 22
Potgieter, Andries 31, 33, 45, 48, 73
Pratt, David 164, *164*
Pretoria 60, *60*, 74, *74*, *75*, 78, 89,
  91, 95, 103, 112, 116, *117*,
  152, *165*
Pretorius, Andries 33, *33*, 38-39,
  42, 43, 45, 48
Pretorius, Martinus Wessel 48, *48*,
  52, 60
Purified National Party 139, 140

Race Classification Board 156
railways 168
  Benguela Railway 176
  Delagoa Bay Railway 60, 63,
    82, 106
  diamond fields 55
  strike (1914) 118, *118*, *119*, 122
Rajbansi, Amichand 184
Rebellion (1914) 120-21, *120-21*, 125
'Reef War' 195, 202
RENAMO movement,
  Mozambique 168, 178
Republic, creation of 163-65, *165*
Retief, Piet 23, 24, 30, 33, *33*, 34,
  34, *35*, 39
Reunited National Party 140
Rhodes, Cecil 52, 55, 57, *57*, 82,
  83, 84, *84-88*, 87, 88, *88*, 89,
  90, *91*, 94, 122
Roberts, Field-Marshal Lord
  Frederick 97, *97*, 100, *101*,
  103, *103*, *104*, 106, 108
Roberts, Lieutenant Frederick 96,
  98
Rome agreement 178
Roodie, Dr Eschel *182*
Rorke's Drift, 64, 68, *68*
'Rubicon address' 187

Sanctions 187, 191, 198

Savimbi, Jonas 176, *176*
Schoeman, Stephanus 48
Schreiner, W P 117, *118*
Second World War 140
  East African Campaign 143,
    143, *144*, 145
  Egypt *124*
  Italy 143, *146-49*, 147-48
  Madagascar 143, 144
  North Africa 143, 144, *144-45*,
    145, 147
Seitz, Dr 126, *127*
Sekhukhuni, Pedi chieftain 60, *60*,
  61, 63
Selborne, Lord 116
Seme, Pixley 139
Separate Amenities Act (1953)
  156, *156*, 158, 195
Shaka, Zulu king 22, 25, 27, *27*,
  68, 72
Sharpeville massacre (1960) 164,
  166, *166*, *171*, 172
Shepstone, Sir Theophilus 60, 63,
  64
Simonstown 116
Slagter's Nek Rebellion (1815) 21
slaves 15, 16, *17*, *18*, 28, 30, *30*, 49
Smit, Erasmus 33
Smith, Captain 42, *42*
Smith, Colonel Sir Harry 45, *46*
Smuts, Jan 51, 105, 109, 111, 118,
  121, *122-24*, 124, 125, *125*,
  126, 128, 129, 131, 132, 134,
  139, 140, 141, *141*, 142,
  152-53
Sobukwe, Robert 170, 172, *172*
Somerset, Lord Charles 21, *21*
South African Communist Party
  (SACP) 192, 201
South African Defence Force
  (SADF) 182, 191
  in Angola 175, *175*, 176, *177*,
    178, Mozambique 178,
    Namibia 179
South African Native Labour
  Contingent (SANLC) 131
South African Races Congress 118
South African Republic 46, 52, 60,
  73, 82, 87
South West Africa 164, 172
  Campaign (1915) *114-15*, 120,
    125-26, *125-27*, 131
South West African People's
  Organisation (SWAPO) 174,
  179, 180
Soweto *185*, *194*, *201*
  unrest (1976) *154-55*, 168, *169*,
    174, 182
Steyn, President Marthinus 74,
  100, 105, 106, 110
Strijdom, J G *157*, 159, *159*, 192
sugar plantations 49, *49*, 51, *135*
Swart, C R *157*, 165, *165*
Swaziland 166, 168

Tambo, Oliver *174*
Terre'Blanche, Eugene *183*, *191*,
  203, 204
Theron, Dr Erika 182
Tjongarero, Daniel *179*
Tomlinson Commission (1954)
  160-62, *160*, 188
Tongaland 72
Torch Commando movement *158*
Transitional Executive Council
  (TEC) 203, 205
Transorangia 31, 33, 45
Transvaal 10, 45, 48, 116, 122, 142
  annexation by British 60, *60-63*,
    64, 73, 75, 84, reversal of 79,
    80
  First Anglo-Boer War 79
  gold mining 55, 82-83, *83*
  Great Trek 31, 33
  Indian immigrants 51, 153
  Jameson Raid 74, 88-89, 91, 92
  Republic, in favour of 164
  Second Anglo-Boer War 103,
    105, 106, 110, 112
Tregardt, Louis 31, *31*
trekboers 18, 28, 73
Treurnicht, Dr Andries *183*, 184
Tutu, Desmond *184*, *191*

United Democratic Front (UDF)
  186, 188, *190*, 191
Uitenhage 186, *187*
Uitlanders 82-83, 88, 89, 122

Ulundi (1879) 70-72, *70*, *71*
Umkhonto we Swize (Spear of the
  Nation) 172, *172*, 187, 201
Union Defence Force 119, 120
  First World War
    Belgium 130, East African
      Campaign 128-29, *128-29*,
      Egypt 130, France 130-31,
      130-31, South West Africa
      Campaign *114-15*, 120,
      125-26, *125-27*
    Second World War
      East Africa 143, *143*, *144*, Italy
        143, *146-49*, 147-48,
        Madagascar 143, 144, North
        Africa 143, 144, *144-45*, 145
Union of South Africa
  creation of 116-18, *116*, 124
UNITA movement, Angola 168,
  175, 176, *176*, *177*, 180
United Nations 124, 166, 168, 178,
  180
United Party 139, *152*, 153, 159
Uys, Pieter 31, 33, 36

van der Stel, Simon 16
van der Stel, Willem Adriaan 16,
  17, *17*, 18
van Deventer, General Jacobus
  120, 128, 129
van Riebeeck, Jan 14-15, *14*, *15*
Verwoerd, H F *157*, 159, 160, *160*,
  161, 163, *163*, 164, *164*, 165,
  166
Viljoen, General Constand 202,
  204, 205
von Lettow-Vorbeck, General
  Paul 128-29, *129*
Vorster, B J 141, 161, 167, *167*,
  168, 182

Waterboer, Nikolaas 52, *52*
White, Sir George 93, 94, 95
'Wind of Change' speech (1960)
  163-64, 166
Witwatersrand gold 'reef' 74,
  82-83, *190*, 191, *see also*
  'Reef War'
Wolseley, General Sir Garnet 63,
  70, *70*, 72
Wood, Sir Evelyn 65, 68, *69*, 80,
  80
World War I & II *see* First World
  War, Second World War

Xhosa tribes 18, 19, 21, *21*, 28, *28*,
  29, 186, 188, *204*, 205, 206

Zaire 168
Zambia 166, 168, 174
Zulus 22, 24, 25, *26*, 27, 33, 34,
  36, *36*, 38-39, 42, 63, *186*,
  187, 188, War (1879) 64-65,
  65-72, 68, 70-72, 186, 188,
  191, *194*, *195*, 201-6
Zimbabwe 167, 168, 178
Zwelethini, King Goodwill 201,
  204, 205

ACKNOWLEDGEMENTS

The author and publishers would
like to thank Design 23 for
designing this book and Pat
Coward for the index. The
following agencies provided
photographic material:

**Africana Museum,
Johannesburg, pages:** 7(bottom),
16, 20(top), 28(bottom), 29(top),
30(top), 31, 32(both), 36-37,
45(bottom), 46(middle), 51(middle),
54(top & bottom right), 70(bottom),
71(top), 73(bottom), 75(bottom),
79(left), 81(top), 82(top), 83(both),
98, 103(bottom right), 153.
Archiv Gerstenberg, pages: 1,
139(both).
Camera Press, pages:
123(bottom), 137, 151(both),
152(top), 157(top), 160(both),
161(below), 162(top), 163(below),
166(top), 167(below), 168(below),
169(below), 171, 172(below),
173(top), 174(all 3), 175(top),
180(bottom), 181(top), 182(below
right), 183(all 3), 185(below).
Cape Archives, pages:
15(bottom)M117/1, 17(top
both)M375 and M139,
18(bottom)M166, 19(left)M342, 23
M473, 28(top)7E, 29(bottom)
E4276, 33(top)E332/2,
36(left)E4274, 38 E328, 40-41
M675, 43(bottom)M487,
45(top)AG8101, 48(bottom), 52, 56
M277 & M709, 60(bottom)M660,
61(Main pix)M684, (inset) E392,
70(top left), 73(top left),
76(top)M1699 & (bottom)M703, 77
E3903, 80(top)M689, 81(bottom)
E4253, 88(top left)AG15368,
101(bottom left) 105(bottom)
AG1234, 108(top)AG13792,
113(top)E8208 & (bottom)M668.
**De Beers Consolidated Mines,
page:** 134.
William Fehr Collection, pages:
2-3, 12(bottom), 13, 14(top),
20(bottom), 48(top), 58-59.
Greenwall Collection, pages:
74(top), 88(bottom right),
89(bottom), 91, 92(both), 93(top &
bottom right), 94(top), 96(all),
100(bottom), 103(bottom left),
106(top), 107(both), 109(both),
110(both), 111(bottom).
Hulton-Deutsch, pages: 24(top
left), 55(both), 56(both), 64(both),
68(bottom), 69(bottom), 70(top
right), 72(all 3), 73(above right),
76(middle), 79(right), 80(bottom),
86, 87(bottom), 90(top right &
bottom), 94(bottom), 95(right),
97(bottom), 100(top), 101(top), 116,
117(top), 118(top left & bottom),
119(bottom), 121(top 2), 122,
123(top), 128-129, 158(below).
Illustrated London News, pages:
90(top left), 121(bottom), 126(left),
131.
Robert Hunt Library, pages: 114-
115, 125(both), 126(right), 127(top),
130, 144(centre), 146, 147,
156(top), 170(top).
**Collection Johannesburg Art
Gallery, page:** 141(right).
The Keystone Collection:
117(bottom), 129(top), 142(both),
143(both), 144(top & bottom),
150(below), 156(below), 158(top),
159(below), 162(below),
166(centre), 176(left), 179(below).
Library of Parliament, pages:
39(top), 85.
**Local History Museum
Collection, Durban, pages:** 6-7,
22(bottom, both), 33(middle),
34(bottom), 42(both), 44(bottom),
49(all 3), 50(both), 51(top &
bottom), 65(bottom), 66-67.
Mansell Collection, pages:
21(bottom), 120.
McGregor Museum, page:
87(top).
Peter Newark's Historical

Pictures, pages: 10(bottom),
12(top), 26, 35, 53, 54(bottom left),
65(top) 69(top), 78, 89(top),
93(bottom left), 101(bottom right),
102(top), 124(bottom).
Pix Features, pages: 10(top),
19(right), 22(top), 27, 33(bottom),
46(bottom), 47(both), 99, 118(top
right), 124(top), 127(bottom), 132,
133(both), 138, 141(left),
157(below), 161(top), 163(top),
167(top), 168(top), 169(top),
175(below), 177(top), 179(top),
181(top), 182(top), 185(top).
Reuters/Bettmann, pages:
180(top), 186, 187, 188, 189,
190(both), 191, 192, 193(both),
194(both), 195, 196, 197, 198,
199(both), 200, 201(both),
202(both), 203(both), 204, 205,
206(both).
**Royal Commonwealth Society,
pages:** 135(both), 136.
South Africa Library, pages: 6,
7(top), 8-9, 11(both), 14(bottom),
15(top), 17(bottom), 18(top),
21(top), 24(top right & bottom),
25(both), 30(bottom), 34(top),
39(bottom), 43(top), 44(top),
46(top), 68(top), 71(bottom),
74(bottom), 75(top), 82(bottom),
111(top), 112(all 3).
**Courtesy South African Museum
of Military History, pages:** 140,
145, 148, 149(both), 150(below).
Frank Spooner Pictures, pages:
154-155, 176(right), 177(below),
178(top), 182(left).
Topham Picture Library, pages:
119(bottom), 152(below), 159(top),
164(both), 165(both), 166(below),
170(below), 172(left & right),
173(bottom), 178(below),
184(below).
Weidenfeld Archive, pages:
88(top right), 95(left), 102(both),
103(top), 104(both), 106(bottom),
108(bottom)/Africana Museum,
60(top)/Illustrated London News,
97(top)/Rhodes Museum, 84(top).